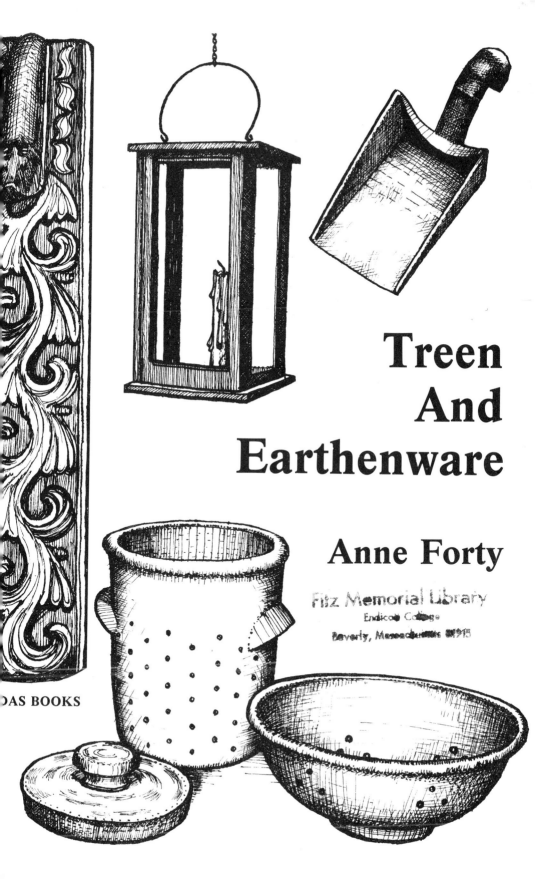

Treen
And
Earthenware

Anne Forty

DAS BOOKS

The Illustrator

Chris Addison was born in London in 1939. He was evacuated to Budleigh Salterton in Devon, where he stayed until the end of the war. He returned to school in London to study painting at the Camberwell School of Arts and Crafts under Gilbert Spencer, and subsequently Robert Medley. After National Service he went to Leeds to complete a teaching course, and recently spent a year at Goldsmith's College. He now lives, with his wife and three daughters, close to the Ashdown Forest in rural Sussex successfully combining teaching, painting and making various musical instruments. He has a love of traditional folksong and music, which is a constant source of interest, inspiration and enjoyment to him.

General Editor: Brian Jewell
In the same Midas Collectors' Library
Smoothing Irons
Veteran Talking Machines
Motor Badges and Figureheads
Veteran Scales and Balances
Teapots and Coffee Pots
Early Typewriters

First published 1979 by
MIDAS BOOKS
12, Dene Way, Speldhurst
Tunbridge Wells, Kent TN3 0NX

© Ann Forty 1979
ISBN 0 85936 074 1

Typeset & Artwork by VDU Characters, 77A High Street, Edenbridge, Kent.
Printed and bound in Great Britain
at The Pitman Press, Bath.

Contents

A   Earthenware Brandy Container

B.   Cheese Print. A carved wooden board for impressing a design on cheese. This example is the Royal Stuart print

INTRODUCTION

Although treen and earthenware are not as readily available as they used to be before everyone caught the collecting 'bug', the interested and enthusiastic newcomer will still be able to find plenty of pieces to start off their collections. Every visit to a new area, whatever the original purpose, will inevitably end up as a tour of the antique shops, in anticipation of a new find.

This book does not attempt to be a definitive work on either treen or earthenware. It is written solely as a guide for the new collector, who has little knowledge of the two subjects, in the hope that it will be of some assistance to them

Of course it is very difficult to know whether an article is genuine or not, and even the experienced collectors make mistakes. Until one has studied and gained experience, the best plan is to find an accommodating and reliable dealer who would be prepared to help, and when in doubt ask his advice.

For those wishing to delve more deeply into these subjects, I have included a select bibliography. I am sure you will find reading these books both fascinating and absorbing.

I hope I have provided some useful guidelines and wish you good hunting.

Bradford, 1978   A.F.

A Pole Lathe. From a seventeenth century Dutch engraving

1 TREEN
History

The dictionary definition of treen merely states 'made of tree — wooden'. This is, of course, true but does not really explain it sufficiently. Treen is the old English word for trees — the 'n' taking the place of the 's' in the plural. Originally treen referred only to platters, bowls, drinking vessels and spoons but over the years has come to cover most small wooden domestic and farm utensils, and preceded pewter as pewter preceded earthenware.

The first wooden articles were made almost straight from the tree and were very basic; in rural areas where people were quite isolated, they were obliged to make their utensils from whatever material was close to hand and wood was the most common. Very few pieces of treen are to be found dating from earlier than the sixteenth century, most of it is from the eighteenth or nineteenth centuries. When one considers that it had little intrinsic value it is surprising that so much treen has survived at all.

The artisan needed no training, just a piece of wood and a knife. Many country folk whittled during the long dark winter nights and the rustic love tokens bear witness to this. Considering the effort involved, after a very laborious day, working by rush light — they really are a labour of love.

The invention of the pole lathe in the Middle Ages meant that, from that time on, the majority of treen pieces were turned. A good description of the turner's work is by Dr Iorwerth C. Peate in *Guide to the Collection illustrating Welsh Folk Crafts and Industries*:

'The tools used by these turners are simple hook tools, which are made by the turners themselves, the correct tempering of the metal being considered a fine art. The cutting end of each tool is curved round into a semi circle, the one tool being used for the hollowing of the vessel turned, and the other for the shaping of the outside of the vessel. With continuous motion in the work, as in the ordinary lathe, the tendency is for the tool to become fixed or clogged by the accumulation of shavings, so rendering the tools unmanageable. In this respect, therefore, the intermittent motion of the pole lathe is valuable, since the tools cut on the down stroke only: the up stroke, being against the tool, cleans away the shavings . . . the adjustability of this pole lathe rest gives such an angle that the tool can be worked "with the grain" and so prevent the scraping of the surfaces of the turned vessel.'

The country kitchen of the Middle Ages was the hub of the house. Besides catering for those living in it, it also provided hospitality for any visitors. The houseproud woman of yesteryear was farseeing and economical. Any surplus food was preserved for future use. Butter was laid down for the winter months; apples peeled, cored, cut into rings and threaded on strings to dry; eggs were pickled; grapes dried; nuts stored in jars and herbs tied in bunches to dry. There were many treen articles in the kitchen supplied by the turner and the cooper. Most small towns and quite a number of villages had a cooper. He made and sold a wide variety of domestic utensils such as tubs and vats for storing and salting, churns and casks, sieves and strainers, flour bins, bowls, ladles, and scoops, to name a few. These were all the accoutrements of the good housekeeper. No kitchen would have been complete without its spice boxes, mills, candle and tinder boxes, spoon and pipe racks.

The cooper also made quantities of farm utensils, sieves and riddles, shovels and shauls, kegs and barrels, costrels or firkins, chicken coops, wedges, taps and stools. In the north of England there were even travelling coopers who journeyed from place to place carrying their tools on their backs. A cooper's sign over a shop in Hailsham, Sussex, said:

'As other people have a sign
I say — just stop and look at mine!
Here Wratten, cooper, lives and makes
Ox bows, trug baskets and hay rakes,
Sells shovels, both for flour and corn
And shauls, and makes a good box churn.
Ladles, dishes, spoons or skimmers,
Trenchers too, for use at dinners.
I make and mend both tub and cask
And hoop 'em strong to make them last.
Here's butter prints and butter scales,
And butter boards and milking pails.
N'on this my friends may safely rest
In serving them I'll do my best;
Then all that buy, I'll use them well
Because I make my goods to sell.'

At the other end of the scale in the great houses of the Middle Ages, master, mistress, visitors and retainers all dined in the Great Hall. The former had chairs and sat at the 'high table', so called because it was on a raised platform overlooking the rest of the hall. Drinking vessels, trenchers, a knife and a spoon were provided.

At the lower tables trenchers were often shared by two people and large bowls were used communally, everyone helping themselves with their hands. Knives were not provided, as all ordinary folk carried their own in a sheath attached to their belts.

Farming Treen

A

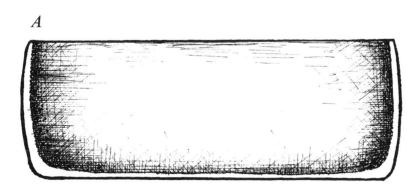

B

A. Seed Lip
B. Scoops

Farming Treen

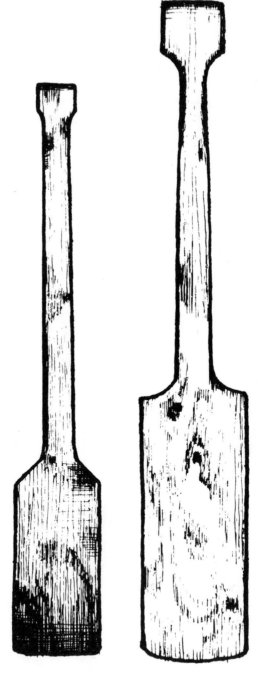

Snow Spades

Farming Treen

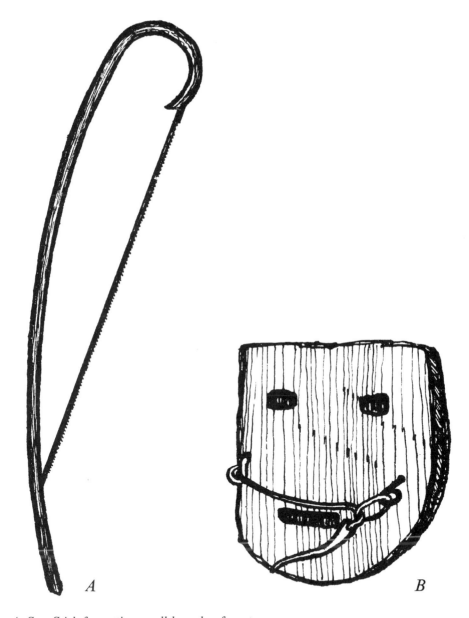

A. Saw Stick for cutting small branches from trees
B. Horse Mud Shoes: wooden shoes with iron staples to enable horses to move more easily in swamps. American

Farming Treen

Malt Shovel and Fork, also known as Barley Shovels, used in nineteenth century mills. These examples are broader than average

Farming Treen

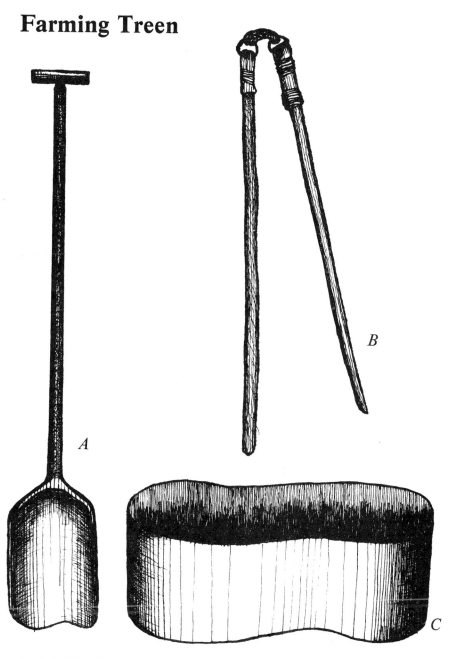

A. Grain Shovel
B. Flail for threshing grain. The hazel or ash handle is held whilst swinging the
   shorter stick or swingel — the part that threshes the corn
C. Corn Shaul

Dairy Treen

Egg Box of the Dairy Outfit Co Ltd, Kings Cross. 1900-1920 period

Dairy Treen

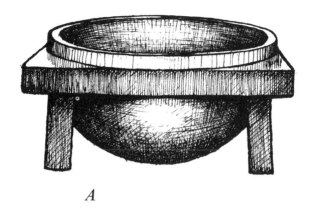

A

B

A. *English turned Whey Bowl in elm. The bowl and block are made from one piece and the feet inserted.*
B. *Hexagonal Butter Mould from Maine, USA*

Dairy Treen

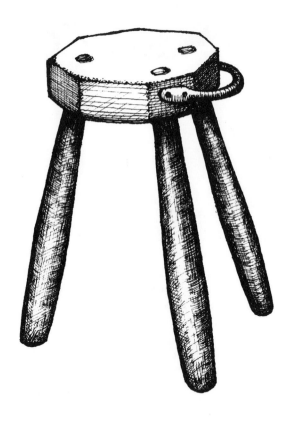

Milking Stool with handle

Dairy Treen

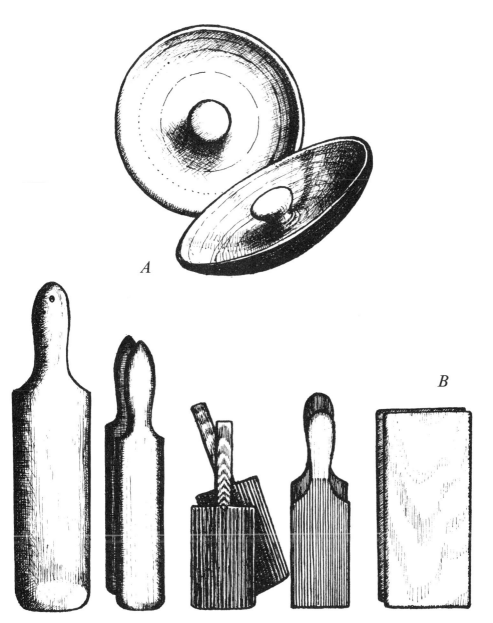

A. Butter Workers to squeeze the water out of butter by hand
B. Butter Pats for shaping butter into oblong pats

Dairy Treen

Barrel Churn

Dairy Treen

Yard of Butter Worker. A mechanical device for squeezing moisture from butter. Invented in 1842 in Connecticut, USA. A revolving ribbed roller travels the length — a yard — of the trough

Dairy Treen

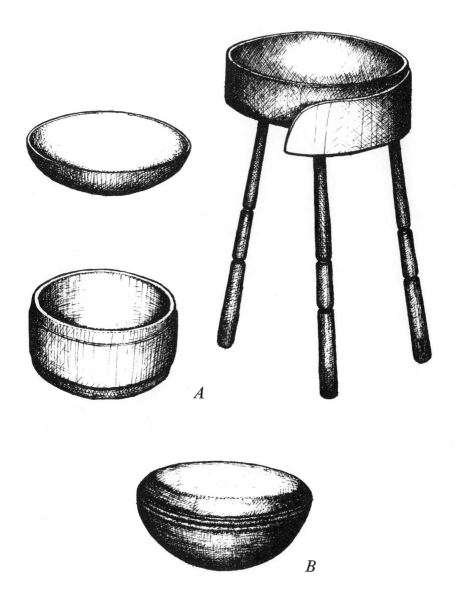

A.

B.

A. *Vats and Dairy Bowls. The Cheese Vats are also known as Chessels. After the cheese had settled in the tub and shrunk away from the sides, it was drained of whey and stored in vats*
B. *A Butter Bowl for taking samples of butter to market*

Dairy Treen

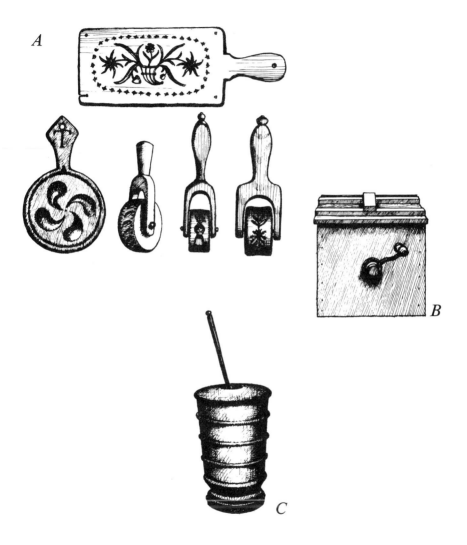

A. Butter Prints. Made in many sizes and patterns. Mostly in sycamore but some in lime and boxwood
B. Box Churn
C. Plunger Churn

Drinking and Eating

The first plates were merely thick squares of bread that soaked up gravy and could be eaten: they were known as tranchers in Normandy and as trenchers in England. Gradually the bread squares were superseded by flat oblong boards, also called trenchers. They were not so effective as, having no edge, the gravy dripped off and it was not long before the boards were given an edge, or had a rounded hollow scooped from the centre.

By the seventeenth century the square trencher had become a round platter. Another form of plate was the roundel, a thin, flat, round wooden platter used by royalty or the very wealthy in the sixteenth and seventeenth centuries for cheese or sweetmeats at the end of a banquet or feast. On the reverse side were painted verses ornately bordered by flowers, ribbons and scrolls. These verses were said, or sung, in turn all around the table and became known as roundelays.

Salt has been one of the most important household commodities, from earliest times. In the royal and noble households the salts were often magnificent examples of the craft of the gold- or silversmith. The squires, farmers and peasants had treen salts and these came in various shapes and sizes. They were made in mahogany, walnut, laburnum, cherry, teak and lignum vitae and many examples have survived.

Treen drinking vessels are more varied and, generally speaking, more valuable than other treen utensils. It is impossible to describe drinking utensils in chronological order as many of them, goblets and tankards for example, were made from earliest times and never became obsolete — they were just made from other materials.

This quote from *Heywood's Philocothonista,* or *The Drunkard Opened (1635)* will give an idea of the types of treen drinking vessels:

'Of drinking cups divers and sundry sorts we have; some of elme, some of box, some of maple, some of holly etc; mazers, broad-mouthed dishes, noggins, whiskins, piggins, crinzes, ale-bowls, wassail bowls, court dishes, tankards, kannes, from a pottle to a pint, from a pint to a gill.'

Wood has always been associated with drinking as it is essential for wine fermenting, presses, vats and casks for brewing. The inns themselves, with their timbered frames, gables, heavy doors and beamed ceilings, were built from wood and inside were full of treen objects: benches, wooden panelling, tables and stools, shelves, casks and tankards. Early tankards were staved and bound with hoops, had lids and handles and held two quarts. Most surviving lidded wooden tankards are Scandinavian. However, the elaborately carved tankards and chalices do not really belong in this book because they are decorative rather than utilitarian pieces.

Table Treen

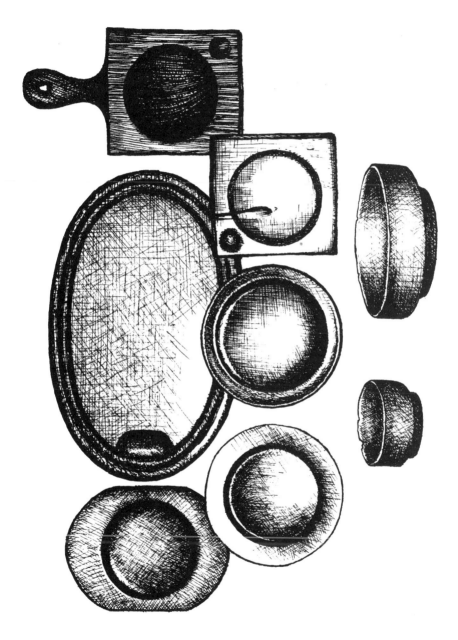

A selection of Platters, Bowls and Trenchers some with salt cavities

Table Treen

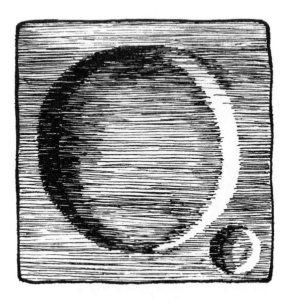

Trenchers. After the use of a slice of bread as a plate came the trencher, an oblong or square board with no edge. Later they were given a scooped out centre. These examples have a small well for salt

Table Treen

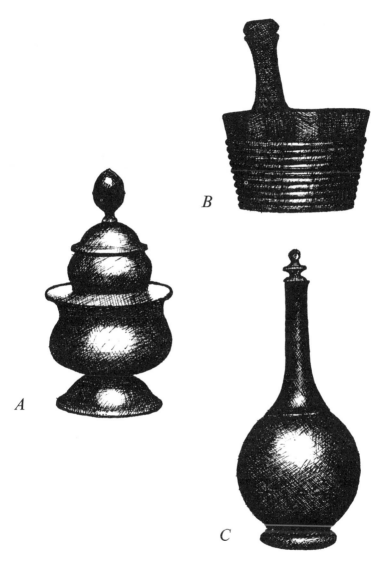

A. *Posset Cup. There is usually a container in the lid for spices and a hollowed out base for the lemon. Posset was a hot spicy drink made from milk, lemon, sugar, spices and ale or wine, taken as a nightcap or as a cure for colds*

B. *A Luggie was used as a ladle for taking ale from a large container. The same vessel was known as a Piggin when used as a milk ladle*

C. *One-piece mulberry wood Decanter*

Table Treen

A. *Treen Goblets are impossible to date with accuracy. They are made in a variety of woods: ash, beech, chestnut, fruitwood, mahogany, oak, walnut and yew*

B. *Beakers. Tapering straight-sided drinking vessels in many different sizes*

The most important of the drinking vessels are mazers. These are shallow, two handled bowls. Edward Pinto says:

'The word mazer appears to be derived from the old German words *masa* meaning a spot or speck (the origin of our measles) and *maserle* the maple tree. Mazer, therefore, originally denoted the speckled wood from which the drinking bowls were made.'

The great monasteries of the Middle Ages had many mazers and an inventory of the monastic houses recorded:

1328	Canterbury	182 mazers
1437	Battle	32 mazers
1446	Durham	49 mazers
1540	Waltham	15 mazers
1540	Westminster	40 mazers

The largest mazer is the Great Mazer of York which is 12⅝ ins diameter; two other important ones are the St Bedes Bowl and the Guy of Warwick mazer.

The communal bowl, intended for holding the drink rather than drinking from it, was introduced in the seventeenth century. This was the wassail bowl, a large bowl for punch or lambswool which had dippers for individual drinks. Lambswool was so called because the beaten egg whites used in the drink caused a froth on top which looked rather like lambswool — so the wassail bowl is sometimes referred to as a lambswool bowl.

It was with the introduction of lignum vitae into England that turners were able to produce a large bowl. It was the only tree then known that was large enough to provide a bowl 15-16ins in diameter without jointing. The smaller wassail bowls had been made since the Saxon period. Although wassailing goes back to pagan times it has mainly become associated with Christmas. In rural areas carol singers carried the bowl through the villages whilst carolling.

There are many references to both the wassail and lambswool made by writers and poets throughout the ages. One of the earliest is a translation from the French *Chronicle of England* by Robert Manning — a Gilbertine canon in the monastery of Brunne, or Bourne, in Lincolnshire — who flourished in the latter part of the reign of Edward I and throughout that of Edward II.

> ' . . . This is their custom and their gest,
> When they are at the ale or feast,
> Ilk man that loves where him think
> Shall say Wassail! and to him drink.
> He that bids shall say Wassail,
> The tother shall again Drinkhail!
> That says Wassail drinks of the cup
> Kissing his fellow he gives it up.
> Drinkhail he says and drinks thereof,
> Kissing him in bourd and skof.
> The King said, as the knight gan ken
> Drinkhail smiling on Rowenen,
> Rowen drank as her list
> And gave the King, syne him kissed.
> There was the first wassail in dede
> And that first of fame gaed.
> Of that wassail men told great tale

'And wassail when they were at ale
And drinkhail to them that drank
Thus was wassail ta'en to thank.'

Strutt, in *Sports and Pastimes of the People of England,* II iv, says:

'Wassail, or rather the wassail bowl, which was a bowl of spiced ale, formerly carried about by young women on New Year's Eve, who went from door to door in their several parishes singing a few couplets of homely verses composed for the purpose, and presented the liquor to the inhabitants of the house where they called, expecting a small gratuity in return . . . '

Robert Herrick also made many references to them in his poems and here are but two:

'. . . I sing of may poles, hock cats, wassails, wakes,
Of bridegrooms, brides, and of their bridal cakes.'

and in *Twelfth Night* or *King and Queen:*

'Next crown the bowl full
With gentle lambs-wool,
Add sugar, nutmeg and ginger
With store of ale, too:
And thus ye must do.
To make a wassail a swinger.

Give them to the King
And Queen wassailing;
And though with ale ye be wet here;
Yet part ye from hence.
As free from offence
As when ye innocent met here.'

Standing cups are, as the name implies, cups with a stem and foot. Even as early as the eleventh century they were a prized possession. Seventeenth century treen standing cups are very rare and therefore expensive. Goblets are smaller versions of standing cups made of ash, beech, sycamore, chestnut, yew, mahogany, oak, olive and walnut.

Loving cups were similar in shape to goblets but slightly larger as they were not used individually but passed round the table so that everyone in turn drank from it.

Many of the drinking vessels are alike in design but vary slightly in size and have different names. For example a piggin and a luggie were both small pail-shaped containers with one stave, longer than the others, used as a handle. Bickers and coggies were straight-sided vessels with two long staves — one at each side — forming handles. Small bickers were used for whisky as were quaichs, a shallow Scottish drinking vessel made in alternate light and dark woods.

Table Treen

Wassailing, now associated with Christmas, began in Saxon times. Carol singers carried the wassail bowl through the streets of villages, to be filled with punch or 'lambswool'

Table Treen

A. Eighteenth century English revolving Cheese Plateau with grooves to help grip the cheese

B. Salts. Salt has been an important commodity since earliest times. In the Middle Ages when Master, Mistress, Guests and retainers ate together the standing salts divided those 'above salt' — the quality: and those 'below salt' — the retainers. These shapes are mainly from the eighteenth century

Table Treen

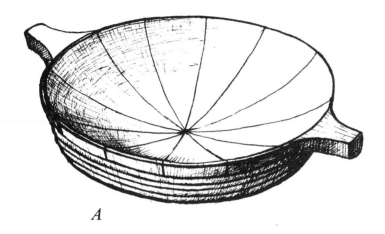

A

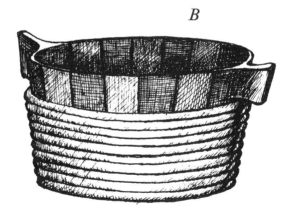

B

A. Quaich. A shallow, two-handled spirit bowl. Larger versions were passed round
   in the manner of a loving cup
B. Bicker. A small Scottish drinking vessel similar to the Quaich, the difference
   being that a bicker had straight sides and a quaich had curved sides. Small
   bickers were for spirits, medium sizes for ale and sometimes as porringers. Really
   large bickers are known as coggies

Table Treen

Salt and Muffiner

Flasks

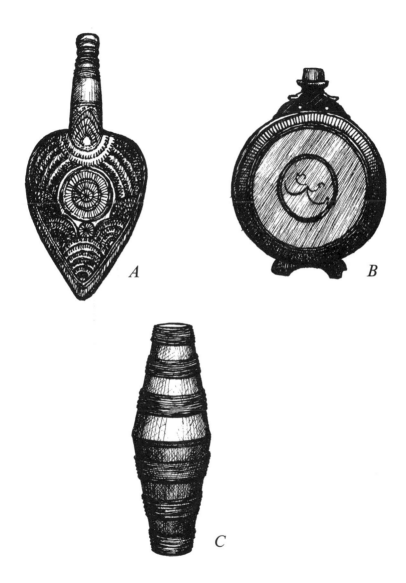

A. Russian soldier's Flask from the Crimean War
B. Water Flask
C. Captain Scott's Flask used in 1899

Kitchen And Larder Treen

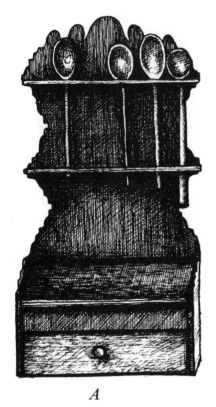

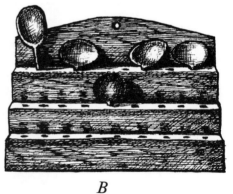

A. *English Spoon Rack and Cutlery Holder. Cottage or farmhouse. Eighteenth century*

B. *Welsh Spoon Rack. Cottage or farmhouse. Eighteenth century*

Kitchen And Larder Treen

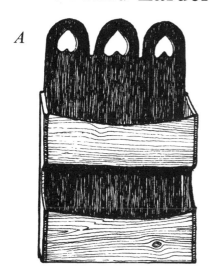

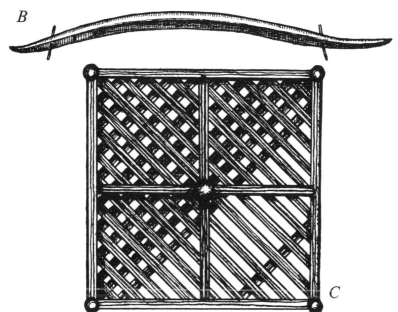

A. *English Double Cutlery Holder. Cottage or farmhouse. Eighteenth century*
B. *American Gambrel. A curved bar for stretching the carcase of a hog or calf*
C. *Bacon Rack. These were also known as Cratches. Suspended from the ceiling by cords for storing bacon. They served the double purpose of keeping the bacon out of reach of rats and mice as well as allowing it to be seasoned by smoke from the fire*

Kitchen And Larder Treen

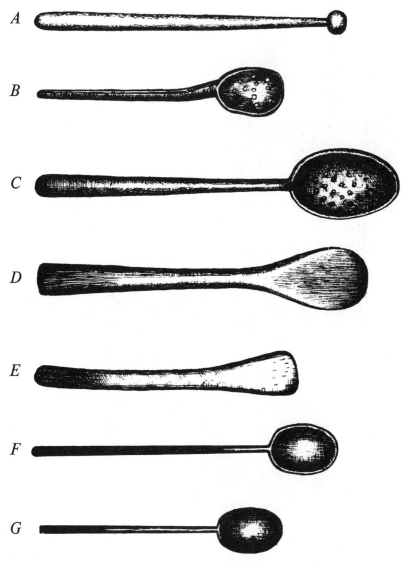

A. *Spurtle for stirring porridge*
B & C. *Strainer Spoons*
D & E. *Spatulas*
F & G. *Kitchen Spoons.*

Kitchen And Larder Treen

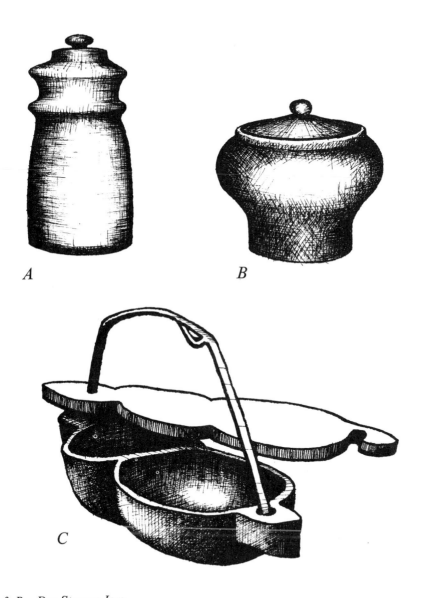

A

B

C

A & B. *Dry Storage Jars*
C. *Salt Boxes. Most Salt Boxes were made to hang in a warm place to keep the salt dry. This was usually near the fire in the kitchen, on the mantlepiece or even in the chimney breast*

Kitchen And Larder Treen

Handled Strainers

Kitchen And Larder Treen

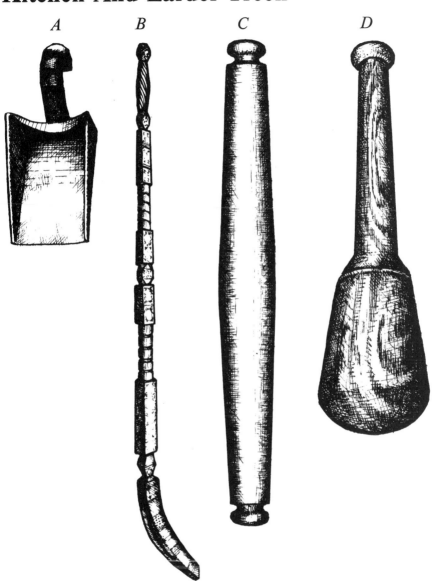

A   B   C   D

A. *Scoop*
B. *Basting Stick used in spit roasting, consisting of a long handle scooped out at the end to form a trough for the fat. This one is inscribed 'This basting stick I give my host to baste his wife for not basting the rost, by me Edward Webster 1646.' Probably Welsh*
C. *Piecrust Roller*
D. *Potato Masher*

Kitchen And Larder Treen

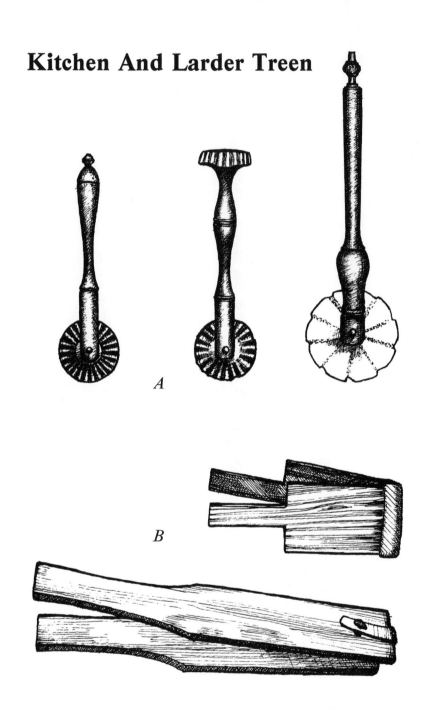

A. *Pastry Markers or Jiggers. Known in the USA as Pie Crimpers*
B. *Lard Pressers. American*

Kitchen And Larder Treen

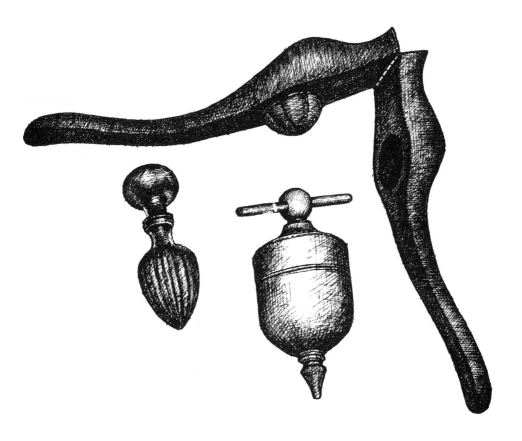

Lemon Squeezers were made from the seventeenth century. These examples are from the eighteenth

Kitchen And Larder Treen

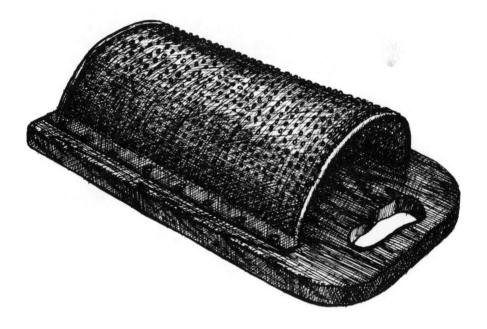

A 'D' kind Kitchen Grater on an oak board

Kitchen And Larder Treen

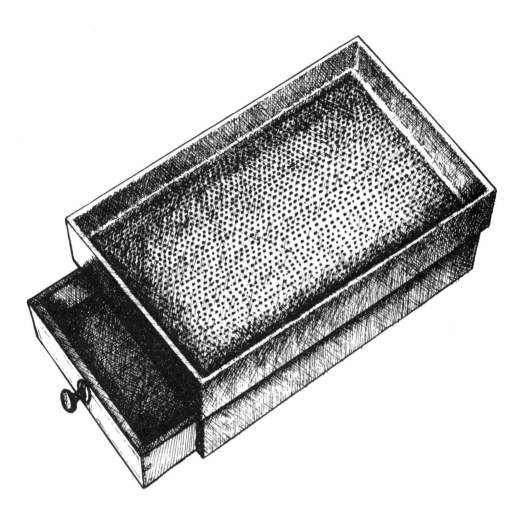

Bread Grater. Until the mid-nineteenth century the blacksmith made graters of sheet iron, with holes punched out, and fixed to a wooden board. This example from Sussex is extra large, made on a pine frame with a crumb drawer

Kitchen And Larder Treen

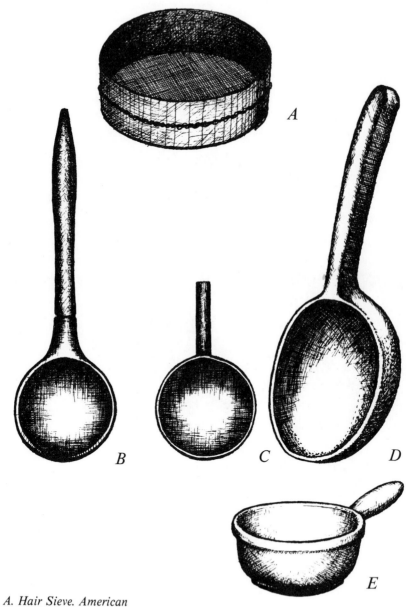

A. Hair Sieve. American
B. Kitchen Ladle
C,D & E. Handled Bowls or ladles.

Kitchen And Larder Treen

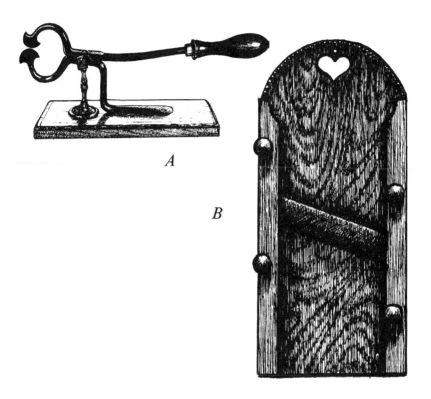

A

B

C

D

A. Sugar Nips. When it came in a loaf, sugar was first broken with a sugar hammer and then broken down for use at the table with either two-handled nippers or a nipper mounted on a wooden stand. Sugar blocks came in many sizes; from 12lbs to 55lbs. They were called sugar cones and if under 12lbs sugar loaves

B. English Vegetable Slicer

C. Welsh Oatmeal Roller or Crusher

D. Scottish or Northern English Oatmeal Roller or Crusher

Kitchen And Larder Treen

A

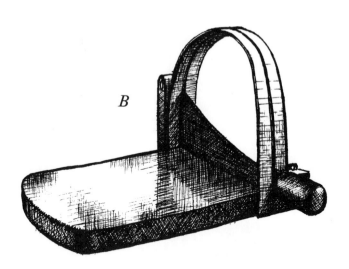

B

Late nineteenth century Bread Slicers:
A. American
B. English

Kitchen And Larder Treen

A

B

A. *Apple Parer. American*
B. *Double-handled nineteenth century Chopper*

Kitchen and Larder Treen

19th century tiered Spice Boxes

Kitchen and Larder Treen

Spice Boxes. As there was no means of storing meat other than by salting, spice was a necessary commodity to cover both the taste and smell of rancid meat in cooking. The sectioned round spice box is from the Regency period. The small round container is Elizabethan and the drawers are German 19th century.

Kitchen And Larder Treen

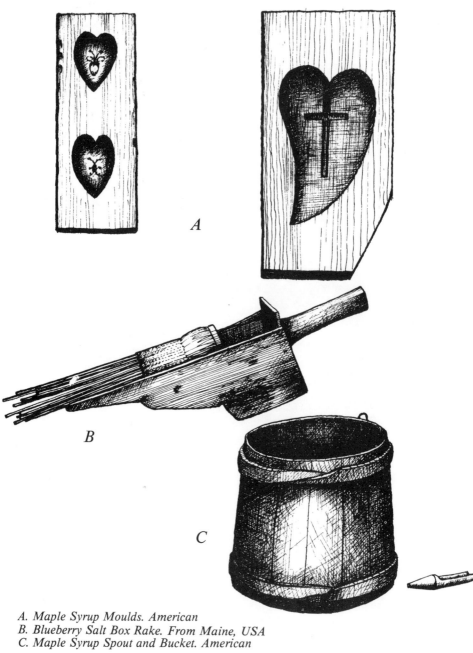

A

B

C

A. Maple Syrup Moulds. American
B. Blueberry Salt Box Rake. From Maine, USA
C. Maple Syrup Spout and Bucket. American

Household Treen

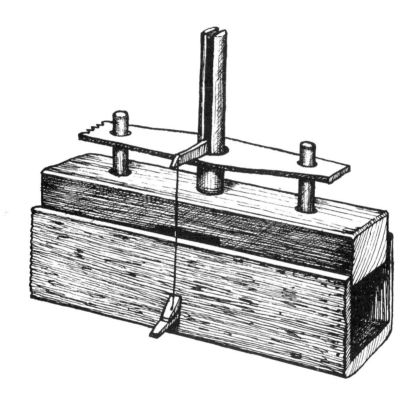

Nineteenth century Rat Trap. 19 ins long

Household Treen

A

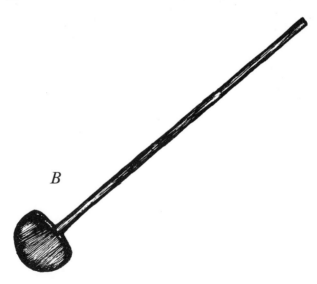

B

A. Bed Wagon. An eighteenth century bed warmer or airer. In the bed the frame
   kept the blankets from touching the hot charcoal smouldering in the pan
B. Feather bed Smoother

Household Treen

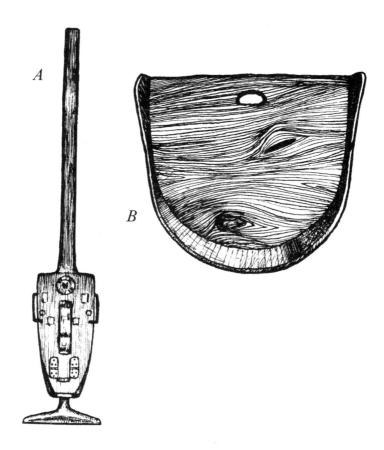

A. The 1913 'Pom' Suction Cleaner made from wood and with leather bellows
B. Kneeling Mat

Household Treen

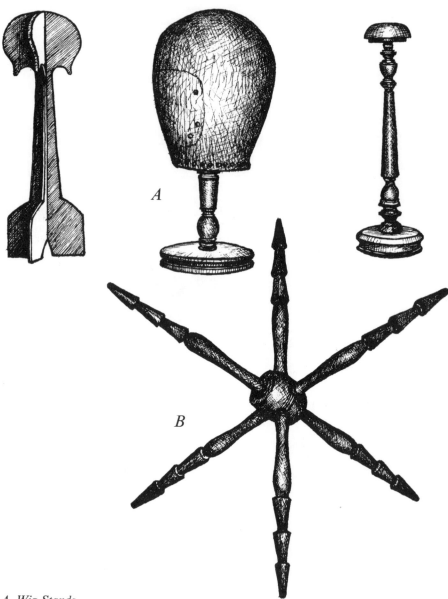

A. Wig Stands
B. Cat. So called because whichever way it fell it landed on its feet. Metal cats were
   used in front of the fire to keep plates and even food warm. Treen cats were for
   holding work boxes or used as flower bowl stands

Household Treen

A

B

A. *Horn Book, also known as a Battledore Book. Used for teaching children the alphabet. Most horn books were made from wood, with lettered paper or parchment protected by a sheet of transparent horn*

B. *Back Board. Used by Victorian children as an aid to good deportment. Held horizontally behind the back, the handles were crooked in the child's elbows, thus holding the shoulders well back*

Laundry Treen

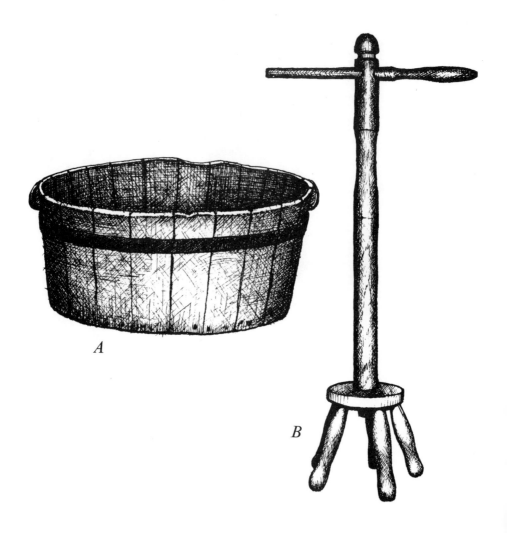

A. *Washing Bowl*
B. *Washing Dolly, also known as a Poss Stick, Dolly Pin or Peggy Stick. Used to pound dirt from clothes*

Laundry Treen

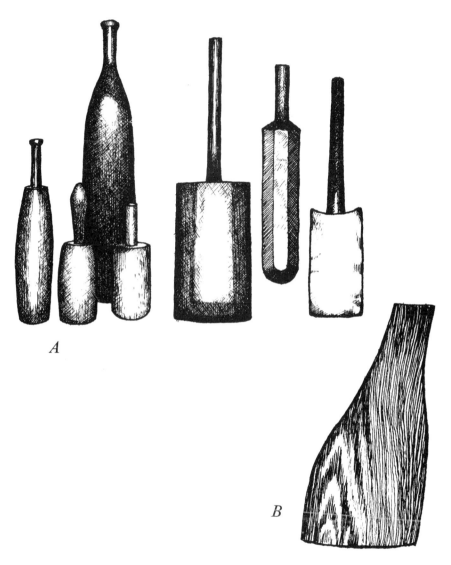

A. *Washing Bats and Beetles. Used in the days when washing was done in the nearest stream. The clothes were placed on stones and beaten with the wooden bats, some of which were ribbed on the face for use as a rubbing board. Beetles were heavy clubs for pounding the dirt out of clothes*
B. *Breeches Board. Used in whitening buckskin breeches. Nineteenth century*

Laundry Treen

Goffering Stack. The damp starched fabric was threaded in and out of the wooden quills, which were held under pressure and secured by wedges. Made from elm c.1800

Laundry Treen

Linen Press. Made in quantity from the seventeenth until the nineteenth century, when linen was pressed before being stored with lavender or herbs. This example is from the nineteen century

Love Tokens

It was a common practice in many countries in Europe for a young man to hand-carve a love token for the young woman he was courting. Their initials, the date, hearts and flowers, were often carved on them. The most usual of the love tokens were the spoon, knitting sheath, stay busk and mangling board.

Sixteenth century spoons are based on the lines of the contemporary pewter and silver ones. Stay busks can be dated from the early seventeenth century when the corset was a necessity in women's formal dress. Knitting sheaths were first made in the mid nineteenth century. The mangling board probably originated in the sixteenth century and was in common use in Scandinavia, Germany and Holland until well into the nineteenth century. They were also taken to far flung places by emigrants and colonists, in particular to the Danish settlements in America, South Africa and Indonesia.

All these love tokens began as a simple present from country boy to his sweetheart but they were copied and elaborated by wood workers as an example of their skill. In the towns, lovers who were not handy with a knife could buy love messages written on pottery or glass or embroidered on a pincushion. Rustic lovers, however, had to convey their feelings in symbolism carved in wood.

The most important love tokens in the British Isles were the Welsh love spoons, which date back to the seventeenth century and the National Museum of Wales has one dated 1667. The date is carved on the hollow handle which contains six small wooden balls divided between the two hollow pillared sections of the stem. At the top of the handle is a circular panel with a heart and geometrical pattern. The initials L. R. and I. W. have been carved on it. These intricately carved spoons offered by a man to a girl later gave rise to the Victorian term 'spooning' meaning courting. All spoons had a ring or hole for hanging them on the wall as a decoration. If a girl was very popular she may have had several love tokens hanging in her cottage. The most popular designs carved were one or sometimes two hearts, chains, keyhole and a comma. The wooden chain symbolized the bonds of marriage, of a heart in chains. The keyhole meant 'the key of my house is yours' whilst the comma, somewhat obscurely, was a 'soul' motif.

Sailors were also prolific with their love tokens, whittling during the long hours on board a sailing ship. Their symbols were anchors, ships, dolphins and chains.

Love Tokens

The earliest existing Welsh Love Spoon, dated 1667, is in the National Museum of Wales
A. *Welsh Love Spoon. c. 1800*
B. *Modern Love Spoons by Charles Jones*
C. *Carved Mangling Board. The prime function was to wring water from clothes. The wet article was wound round a roller which was then rolled backwards and forwards with the mangling board — usually carved and painted as its secondary function was to act as a wall ornament.*

Needlework Treen

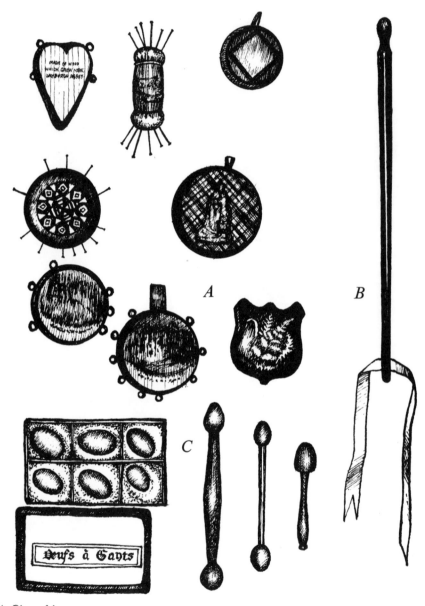

A. Pincushions
B. Ribbon Threader for threading ribbon through slots in garments or through the
   complicated hairstyles of the eighteenth century
C. Glove Darning Eggs

Needlework Treen

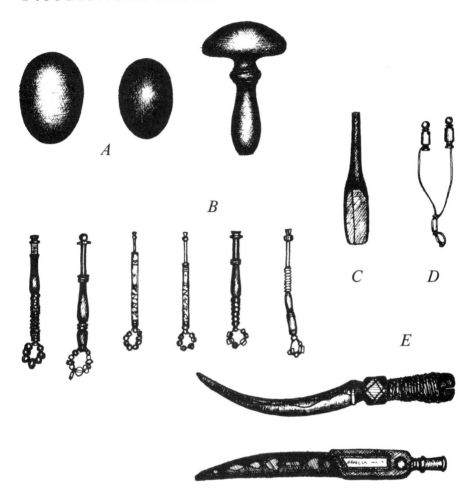

A. Darning Eggs and Mushroom
B. Lace Bobbins. Each area had its own shape. Some had names or messages carved on them and were often used as love tokens, Valentines and as gifts at weddings, funerals and christenings. The coloured beads are not purely ornamental; they weight the bobbin when in use
C. Knitting Broach. A wooden peg round which the wool was wound. The other end was flat and was pushed into the side of a shoe or clog, keeping the wool to hand and free from tangles
D. Knitting Guards. To be placed at the ends of needles to prevent stitches from slipping off
E. Knitting Sheaths. These were worn in a sloping position on the right-hand side to hold the end of the needle; thus taking the weight of the knitting and preventing stitches slipping off double-ended needles

Needlework Treen

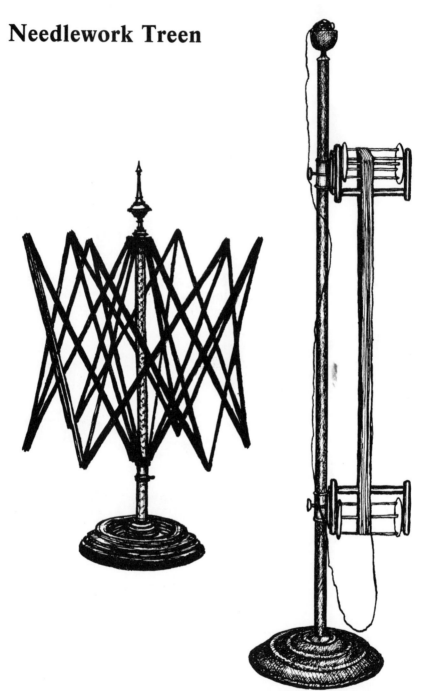

Woolwinders.
That on the left is from the Regency period (Walter Shepherd Collection)

Needlework Treen

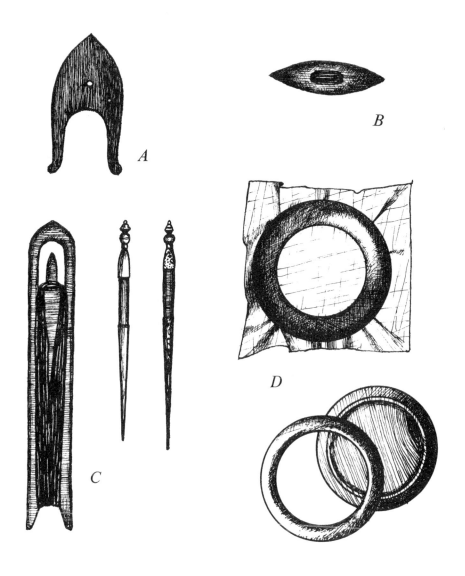

A. *Lucet. Used in cord making in the seventeenth and eighteenth centuries*
B. *Tatting Shuttle. Used in a form of lace making*
C. *Netting Needle and Tools*
D. *Cloth Stretching Frames*

65

Lighting

The first light must have been a firebrand plucked from the fire by cavemen — the only way they could have illuminated their caves in order to paint the murals that have since been found. Oil lamps, which had been used from very early times in some countries, then spread to Europe. These were followed by a soft tallow dip, which was a wick dipped into tallow or any other suitable fat until it was thick enough for the candle holder. Peasants made their own, but in the fourteenth and fifteenth centuries the wealthy in both town and country bought their candles from travelling candlemakers. Wax candles were used in churches and abbeys from very early times and came into wealthy houses in the sixteenth century but were very expensive. At the coronation of King George II Westminster Hall was reputed to have been lit by 1,800 hanging candles and many more on the tables.

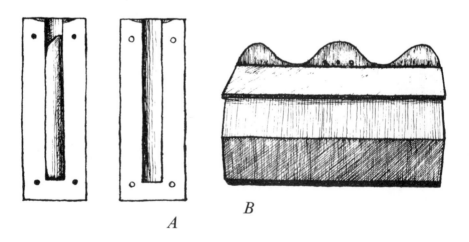

A

B

A. A rare sixteenth century Candle Mould in beechwood. Early moulds were made in two halves and pegged together
B. Candle Box. Candles were expensive and great care was taken of them. English candle boxes were plain and rectangular, made to either hang up or lie flat. Oak and mahogany were the usual woods

Lighting Treen

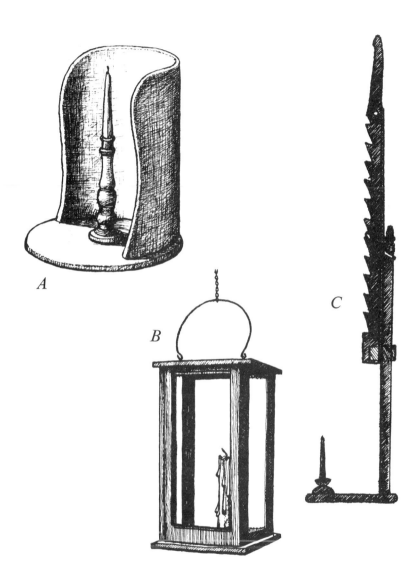

A. Candle Screen. Necessary in draughty rooms. Few were made from wood and those that have survived are from the eighteenth century
B. Lantern or Lanthorn. Until the sixteenth century the panels were of horn. This example is from Alsace; made in the eighteenth century, the panels are of glass
C. Candle Ratchet. A very rare candle holder, dated 1669

Fire Making

For centuries the wood fire was used for heating, cooking and lighting as well as playing an important part in religious ceremonies. It is impossible to put a date as to when early man discovered the method of making a fire at all. No doubt it was a tedious method at first.

Tinder boxes were very inconvenient as any draught or dampness delayed their action. Tinder was usually charred linen pieces, but small pieces of rotten wood, dried grass and leaves were all used.

In 1786 the Phosphorus Box was invented in Italy. This was merely a bottle of phosphorus and matches with sulphur tips. When dipped in the bottle the sulphur ignited.

In 1810 an improved method arrived in England. This was a bottle of sulphuric acid and the matches were tipped with a hard paste made up of sugar, gum and potassium chlorate. These were known as 'Instantaneous Light Contrivances'. Treen boxes are rare but a few examples have survived, these are stamped 'Berry's Patent'.

However, in 1826, John Walker, a chemist from Stockton-on-Tees, invented the first friction lights and sold them at one shilling for 50 which included the piece of sandpaper for rubbing the match head.

Phosphorus matches eventually came to England, from Germany, in 1830 and they became very popular. They were inclined to burst into flame at a knock or if exposed to heat so they were kept at home. The protective matchbox was then invented so that matches could be carried by all.

Fire Making Treen

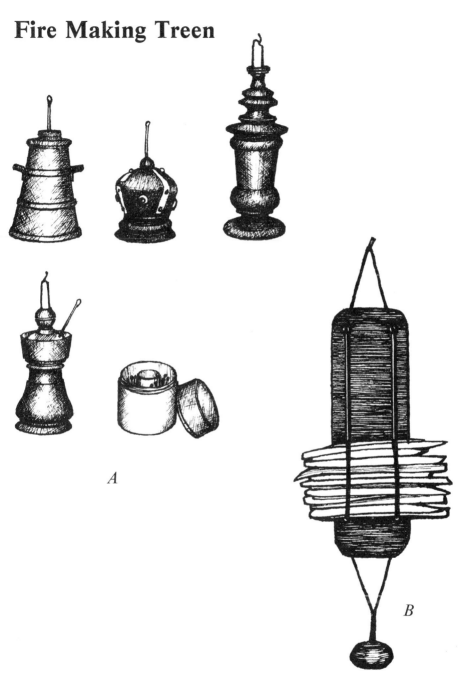

A. Instantaneous Light Devices and Protective Match Boxes ranging in dates
   between 1810 and 1870
B. A Hanging Match Rack in oak. The weight was to keep the cord taut

Pastimes

Wood has been significant in every century for man's amusement or exercise. From maypoles, Punch and Judy, hobby horses, to helter skelters, coconut shies, swings and roundabouts. Children have played with a succession of treen toys — dolls, hoops, building bricks, balls, skittles, kites and jack straws, whilst their parents have played bowls, cricket or croquet. Bowls has been played since the fifteenth century and has always been popular. Tennis was played originally on wooden courts, with wooden rackets. Indoor games abound with draughts, chess and dominoes, bilboquet and tops.

The most common plaything for girls must always have been the doll: from the original rough wooden suggestion of a human figure to the almost life-like models of today, small girls have loved dolls. Of course, in the days prior to the eighteenth century a doll was not considered to be a toy. Children were very much like small adults, dressed like them and were rarely allowed to romp about and play. The 'baby' was given to a small girl so that she became familiar to the ways of motherhood. Boys similarly were given a sword when they came out of their skirts and into the miniature versions of father's clothes.

The real toys were those made by cottagers for their children to play with. They did not have to ape their elders and in some ways had a much gayer childhood than those of the privileged classes.

The main toys were wooden animals, copies of the familiar domestic varieties seen around them, and horses on platforms with wheels to be pulled along. Boats were, simply, hollowed out pieces of wood and slightly made into more elaborate Noah's Arks. Many of these arks were made by French prisoners-of-war during the Napoleonic Wars.

Jack straws — an old wooden version of the now plastic spillikins — was much more attractive than its modern counterpart. Each straw was carved into a shape — saw, crutch, rake, bow, spear, key, axe, ladder, shovel, paddle, rifle, sabre, etc — there are very few treen examples, and those that survive are mainly of bone or ivory.

One of the oldest of games is 'Merels' or 'Nine Men's Morris', said by different authorities to have been brought to England by the Romans, Danes and Normans. Edward Pinto solves the problem by stating, 'Of the three, the Romans must win, on the evidence of a Roman tile, depicting a merels board, excavated at Silchester'.

Cribbage, a very English game, is a card game for two to five people. The cribbage board or markers are very attractive, can be oblong, oval, square or round and are eagerly collected.

Backgammon, which has made a successful 'come-back' in recent years was actually known throughout Asia 1,200 years ago as 'Nard' and at first was called 'Tables' in England. Its name was changed to backgammon in the seventeenth or early eighteenth century.

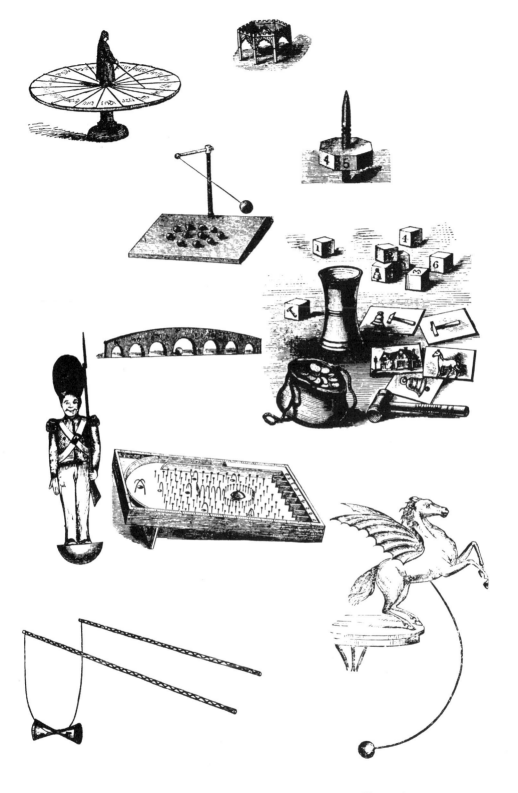

Nineteenth century games in treen from catalogue illustrations

Smoking Treen

A. Pipe Rack and Candle Stick
B. Tobacco Jars

Smoking Treen

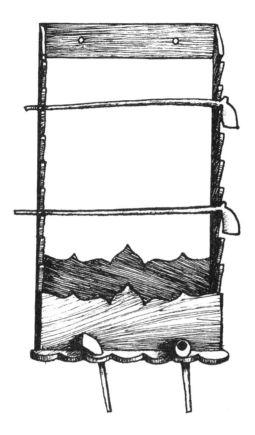

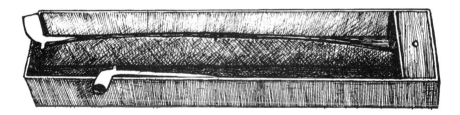

Pipe Racks of the eighteenth and nineteenth century were made to suit all tastes, whether one preferred to store pipes horizontally, vertically, bowls up or down

Tea And Coffee Treen

A

B

C

D

A. *Teapot Stand. Scottish*
B. *Coffee Grinder or Mill. Necessary in England after the introduction of coffee in
the mid-seventeenth century*
C. *Pear Wood Cup and Saucer*
D. *Moustache Cup*

Tea And Coffee Treen

Coffee Grinders or Mills

Tea And Coffee Treen

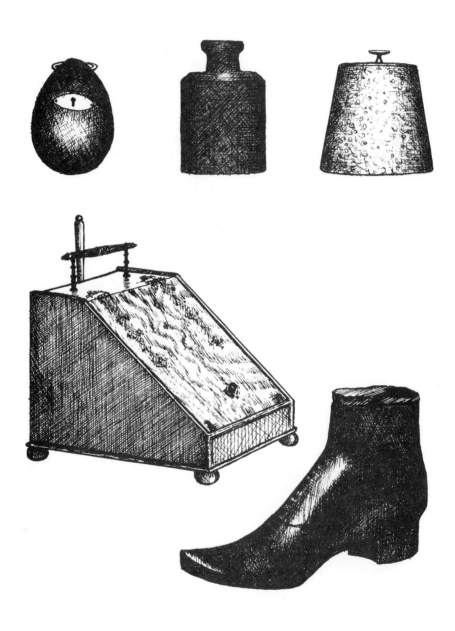

Tea Caddies both plain and novelty

Sticks And Carrying Aids

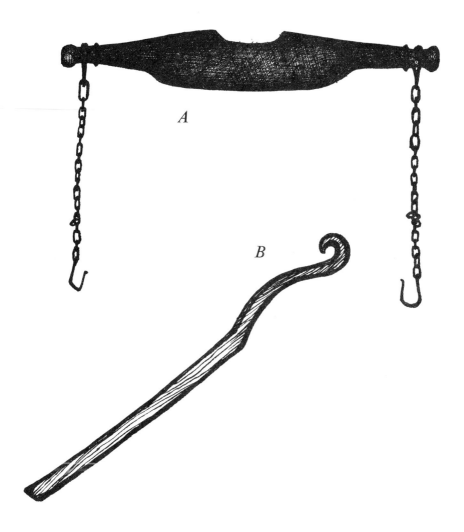

A. Milk or Water Carrying Yoke
B. Pedlar's Pack Stick. Carried across the shoulder with a pack on the curved end.
   In use since the Middle Ages. This example is made from ash and dated c. 1840

Sticks And Carrying Aids

A. Ell Rules. Used for measuring cloth in the nineteenth century. An ell varied in length in different countries; in England it was 45ins, in Scotland 37.2ins, and the Flemish ell was between 26 and 27.5ins.

B. Shepherd's crooks

Sticks And Carrying Aids

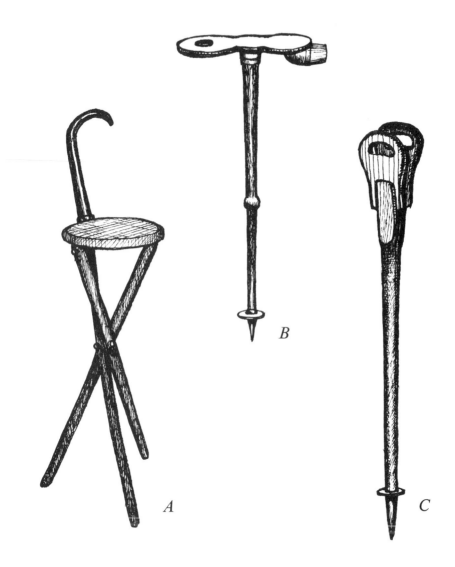

A. Bentwood stick with cane seat. Nineteenth century
B. The seat of this stick unscrews to form a handle
C. All wood predecessor of the modern shooting stick

Industrial Treen

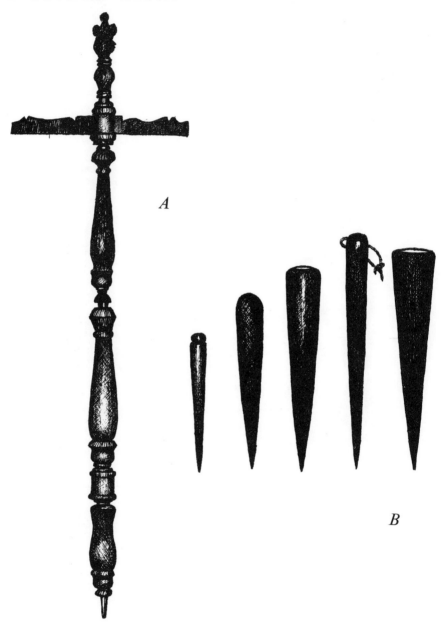

A. *Silk Thrower. Used for spinning and twisting silk thread. This example is Scandinavian*

B. *Fids. Hard wood and carrot-shaped for splicing rope*

Industrial Treen

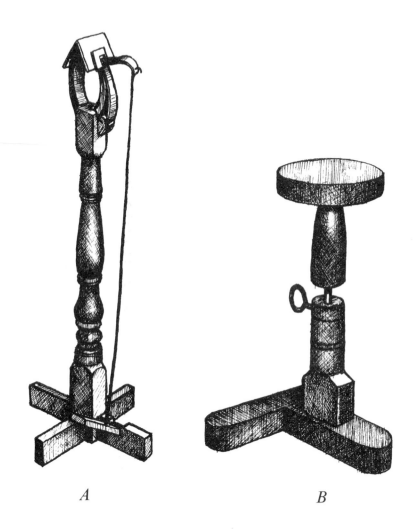

A   *B*

A. *Donkey. A foot-operated clamp for holding gloves whilst stitching*
B. *Potter's Wheel. Two of the oldest machines are the potter's wheel and the lathe.*
   They both revolve the article being made so that both hands are free to work.
   This example is from the eighteenth or early nineteenth century

Offertory And Money Boxes

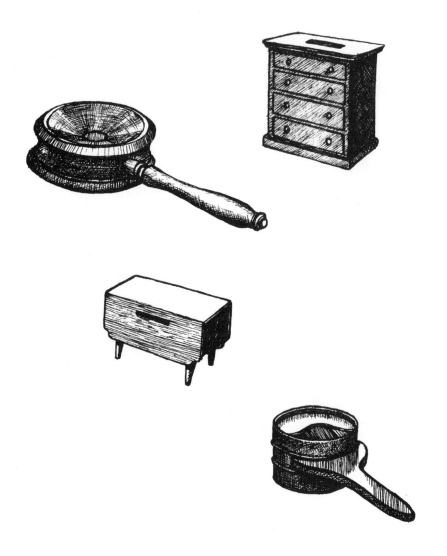

Collecting, Offertory and Money Boxes were made in a wide variety of shapes and sizes in eighteenth and nineteenth centuries

Medicinal Treen

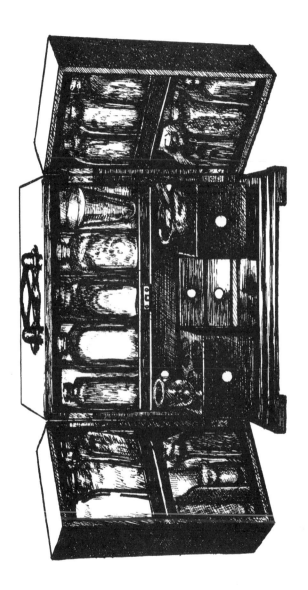

Apothecary Cabinet. Used by chemists and doctors who did their own dispensing. This example carries the label of Ambrose Godfreys, chemist of The Phoenix Head, Southampton Street, Strand, who was active between 1740 and 1777

Medicinal Treen

Phlebotomization Outfit. A box with all the requirements for blood-letting

Medicinal Treen

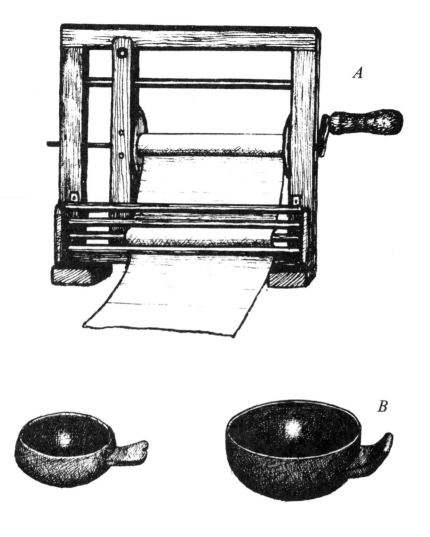

A. *Bandage Winder. Said to have been invented by Florence Nightingale. Nineteenth century.*

B. *Bleeding Bowls.*
   In the fifteenth century barbers also acted as surgeons and continued to practice as blood letters until a separate Company of Surgeons was formed in 1745. The barber's striped pole stems from those times. It was given to the patient to grip during phlebotomization and as it was inclined to become blood stained, it was painted red. When not in use it had a bandage wound round it and used as a sign outside the shop to show that phlebotomy was practiced.

Medicinal Treen

Mortars and Pestles. Small mortars were used mainly by chemists to make up prescriptions. This hexagonal mortar is the earliest known survivor in England, and carries the date 1659 on the base. Height 7½ins

Medicinal Treen

13½ins high Mortar made from walnut

Costrels

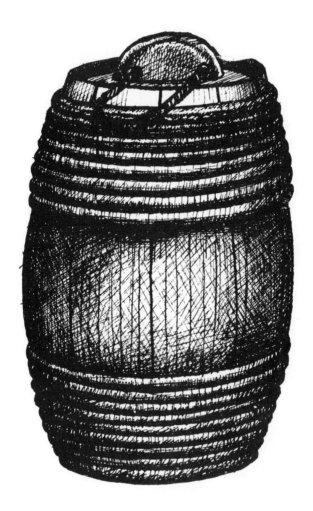

Costrel. A harvest keg also known as a Firkin. This example is of the type used by the Vivandièrs in the Napoleonic Wars

Vivandièr of the 19th century French Army carrying a costrel — a small keg made to hang from the shoulder on a cord or strap.
(Photograph from The Home Headquarters, The Royal Hussars)

Dating Treen

Edward Pinto, in his 'bible' for treen collectors and lovers *Treen and other Wooden Bygones,* explains the difficulties in stating, with any certainty, the date of some treen objects.

'There are four things which are sometimes very difficult to state with certainty about Treen and other wooden bygones. The first is the wood; the second is the date; the third is the purpose for which made and the fourth is why a thing was made of wood rather than some other apparently more suitable material . . . There is only one way of dating wood with any certainty and that, the equivalent of fingerprinting a human, is by microscopic examination of a carefully prepared cut-off section of end grain: to obtain this, without damaging the specimen, is not usually practicable . . . The dating of treen and other small wooden objects is difficult because there are no hallmarks as with silver, touchmarks as on pewter, design books as in furnishing, nor great names among the makers.

'So what have we to go on then? The answer is that there are a few original dated pieces, from which we can assume dates for others of similar design. Trade cards, of which the date is known, sometimes give descriptions and illustrations of the objects made and sold. There are documentary records and descriptions, including some inventories with (although rarely) sketches in the margins, some dated books on turnery showing pictures of objects then fashionable, and a few dated pictures which include treen in their composition. Most valuable for dating are objects with names of makers stamped or engraved on them; where these are London makers, I have been able to establish the addresses and, through them, the dates in a number of cases.

'There are known dates when certain commodities came into vogue and the wooden objects which were then designed for their use or service. There are approximate dates when certain foreign woods were first imported and in the nineteenth century there are trade catalogues. Finally there are the resemblances of certain treen objects to counterparts in silver, pewter, glass and china etc.

'It will be readily realised that there is a large margin for error in some of these aids to dating and possibly most of all the last. This is because treen was sometimes the contemporary, sometimes the ancestor and at other times the country cousin of similar objects in other materials, the latter lagging behind its sophisticated city relations. It must be obvious, therefore, that considerable research and experience are the best guides, but even so the word "probably" should really be inserted before dates, just as it should before woods.'

2 EARTHENWARE
History

There was little pottery made in England in the years between the Roman occupation and the sixteenth century. Of the small amount that was made, the best, technically and artistically, was that produced by the monks of the Cistercian monasteries and was of a plain and well balanced form. It was a hard red-ware, covered with a dark brown glaze and decorated with slip patterns. The patterns on jugs, ewers, plates and bowls are similar to those found in the tapestry, stained glass and paintings of the period.

The term 'Cistercian' ware covers most of the examples found in monastic and ecclesiastical sites and are therefore pre 1540, the date of the Dissolution of the Monasteries. The jug, cooking pot and bowl were the main products of medieval England, and it is not until the reign of Elizabeth I that pottery took a step forward.

The sixteenth century saw the change over from treen drinking and eating vessels to those made of earthenware. This change over meant that small potteries sprang up wherever local clay was suitable, making utilitarian pieces. As the most popular item of earthenware was, at first, the cup, many of the small potteries specialised in cup-making and became known as cuppers. The Potovens area of Yorkshire is the only potting community of this period to have been studied in detail. The kilns were built on the outskirts of Wakefield at Outwood. This was poor agricultural land but well supplied with all the requirements of the potter — clay, water and coal.

A survey in 1608 recorded, 'Certain clay-pits digged by ye cuppers and cup makers inhabiting there' and a further survey in 1709 stated, 'Amongst those who inhabit the cottages on the Outwood is a Manufactory of Earthen Ware Potts of all sorts being made there which require no more than clay and lead'. In a history of Staffordshire published in 1685 by Dr Robert Plot came this description of glazing:

'After the vessels are dry they lead them, with that sort of lead as they call smithum, which is the smallest ore of all, beaten into a dust, finely sifted and strewed upon them; which gives them the gloss . . . they lead them with calcined into powder which they also sift fine and strew upon them as before, which not only gives them a higher gloss, but goes further into them more than lead ore would have done.'

At the beginning of the seventeenth century a pottery was established at Wrotham in Kent. A local red clay was used and the few surviving articles are in the main 'tygs' — a drinking cup with more than three handles. During this period potteries were fairly evenly spread around the country, although they were rather more around the London area.

By the mid seventeenth century the most important potters were those in Burslam, Staffordshire. Instead of each plate being thrown individually on a potters wheel they

"A maker of Dutch-ware at work." A plate from Volume III of *"Spectacle de la Nature"* by N.A. Pluche, translated from the French and published in England in 1740

were now made by rolling clay over domed moulds, which was much quicker. The range of items made in the Potteries from this period onwards was enormous. Not only were these wares made for the home market, large quantities were made for the rest of the British Isles and for export to America. Even in 1635 large amounts of pottery were sent to the New England states and to Maryland and Virginia. Ceramics were made in America, for household use, but were rather primitive, and it was not until after 1812 that the American pottery industry began to flourish.

With the introduction of tea into England came the oriental porcelain teapots, cups and saucers. This created competition within the industry for the better quality wares. As early as 1691 John Dwight was granted a patent for the manufacture of 'Transparent Earthenware commonly known by the names of Porcelain or China' but he was unsuccessful. Astbury and Wedgwood both experimented, trying to imitate the whiteness and finish of the imported porcelain.

By the use of new materials, they developed a ware vastly superior to the common earthenware. But these new methods meant that the cottage industry of pottery had turned into a large scale manufacturing process.

Pancheon

Glossary

Baking Dish: A shallow dish often decorated with trailed slip, used for baking from the eighteenth century.

Barm Pot: A tall straight-sided jar with a rim, for keeping yeast.

Bung-Hole Pot: A pottery cistern which dispensed small amounts of liquid for domestic use from the fifteenth to the nineteenth century.

Butter Pot: A tall straight-sided, unglazed pot for storing butter. By Act of Parliament these butter pots had to weigh less than 6lbs but hold 14lbs of butter.

Caudle Pot: Shaped like a large mug with two handles; Caudle was an oatmeal porridge with spices and wine mixed in it.

Charger: A large shallow plate.

Chicken feeder: A self-filling grain trough for chickens.

Costrel: A small keg made to hang from the shoulder on a cord.

Fire Pot: A round pot with holes pierced around the edge under the rim. It was filled with hot ashes and put under the skirts of lace makers and other sedentary workers to keep them warm.

Fuddling Cup: A trick cup. A number of small cups joined together by handles and channels so that in emptying one the others were also emptied.

Gallipot: A small pot used for ointment.

Gorge: A large jug.

Ham Pan: A pear-shaped pot for salting a whole ham. They usually had a wooden lid.

Lading Pot: A north country straight-sided pot with a handle used for ladling water from boiler to washtub.

Pancheon: A large open pot used when baking.

Piggin: A small pot with a flat handle which protrudes upwards at one side — like the treen piggins — for ladling milk.

Pipkin: A small pot with handles.

Pitchen: A large jug.

Posset Pot: A two handled, lidded pot with a spout, used to drink posset which is a hot milk drink mixed with lemon, spices, sugar and ale or wine.

Pottle: A pot holding four pints.

Salter: A large oval pan used for salting meat.

Salt Kit: A jar with a large circular hand-hole in the side, for storing salt.

Tyg: A mug with three or more handles. Made in all sizes.

Earthenware

Mould — 19th century

Earthenware

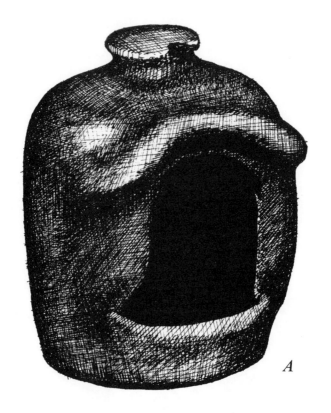

A. *Chicken Feeder*
B. *Ham Pan*

Earthenware

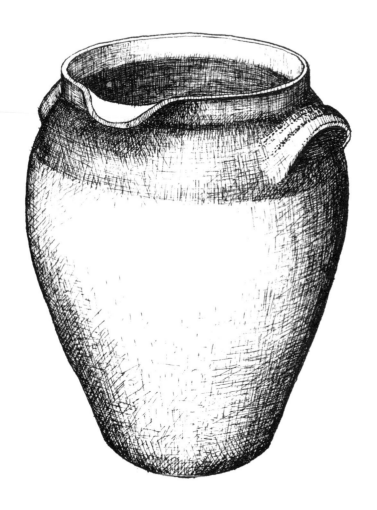

Crock with Lip

Earthenware

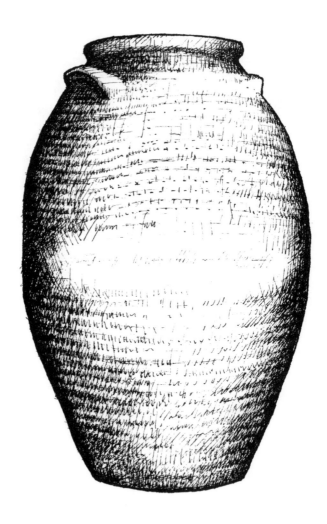

Large Brewing Jar

Earthenware

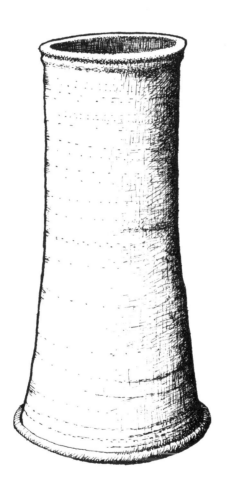

Hand-thrown Chimney Pot.

Earthenware

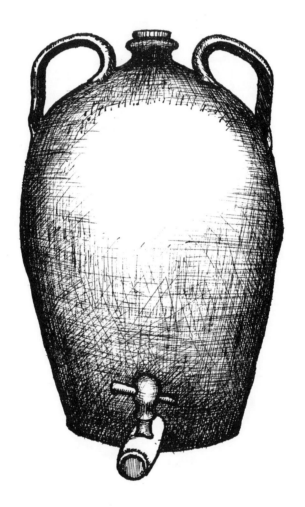

Water Container

Earthenware

Bread Crock

Earthenware

Sink

Earthenware

Bottles

Earthenware

Bottles

Earthenware

Bottle

Earthenware

Halifax Pancheon

Earthenware

Strainers

Earthenware

Salt Kit 19th century

Earthenware

Halifax Salt Kit

Earthenware

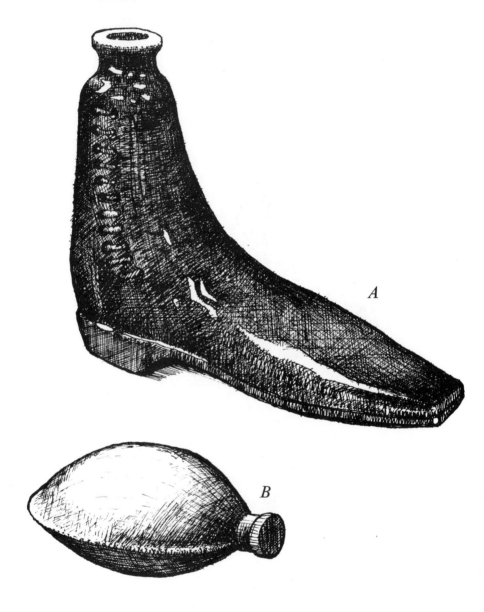

A. *Shoe Warmer*
B. *Handwarmer*

Earthenware

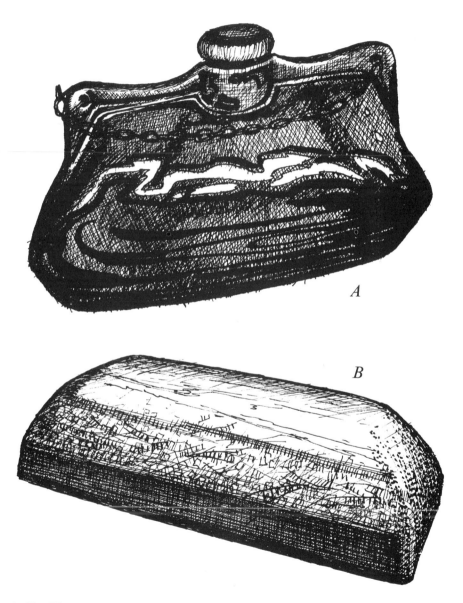

A. Hot Water Bottle
B. Hot Brick

Earthenware

A. Batter Mixer
B. Condensed Milk Container

Earthenware

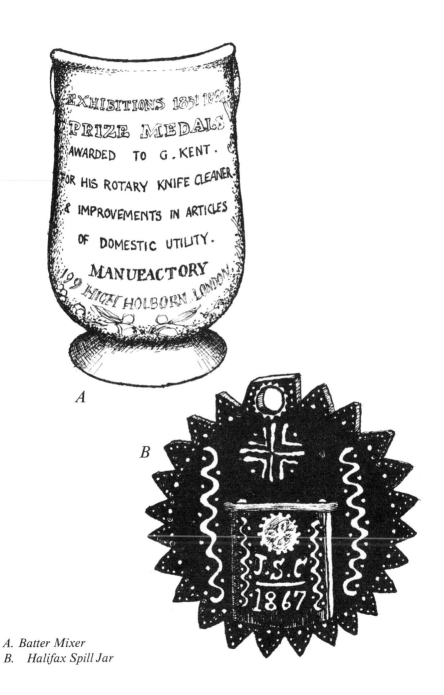

EXHIBITIONS 1851 1862
PRIZE MEDALS
AWARDED TO G. KENT.
FOR HIS ROTARY KNIFE CLEANER
& IMPROVEMENTS IN ARTICLES
OF DOMESTIC UTILITY.
MANUFACTORY
199 HIGH HOLBORN, LONDON.

A

B

J.S.C
1867

A. Batter Mixer
B. Halifax Spill Jar

Types of Earthenware
Delft

Before the introduction of tin-glaze into England in the sixteenth century, English potters had used brown, green and black lead glazes. Tin-glaze was imported from Holland by Jasper Andriss and Jacob Janson, potters from Amsterdam. They petitioned Queen Elizabeth for permission to set up their pottery and use the new technique. First they went to Norwich and had tin brought from Cornwall, this was oxidised and fused with lead oxide and glass. The glaze was then ground and mixed with water into which the fired earthenware was dipped. The porous body soaked up this liquid glaze and the article was then painted and re-fired at a high temperature, in a clay saggar for protection. The word Delft is spelt with a small 'd' when referring to the English ware — it has a capital 'D' when made in Holland.

Creamware and Queensware

A cream coloured earthenware discovered by Thomas Astbury, improved upon by Enoch Booth and developed by Josiah Wedgwood. After he had secured the patronage of Queen Charlotte he re-named it Queensware. Creamware swept the markets at home and abroad and by the end of the century even French manufacturers were turning to it. Its popularity was complete when Catherine the Great ordered the 'Frog' service (so called because it was ordered for La Grenouillere Palace in St Petersburg). It was completed in 1774, decorated with English scenes and cost about £2,250 — in those days an incredible amount of money.

Salt-Glaze Ware

The unglazed ware was fired in the kiln and when the kiln reached its maximum temperature, salt was thrown in, the heat and salt combined to form sodium oxide and hydrochloric acid and formed a hard glaze with a pitted look.

Slip Ware

Slip is potter's clay in liquid form — about the consistency of cream. This was traditionally the method for decorating pottery. The main early centre for slipware was Wrotham in Kent. Early slip-decorated earthenware is very much sought after by collectors.

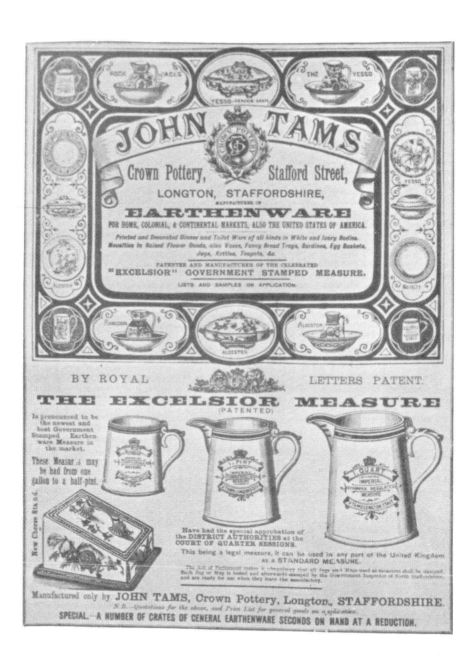

Advertisement from "Pottery Gazette"

Advertisement from "Pottery Gazette"

Directory of Potteries

John Adams
The Adams family have been potters from the reign of Edward I and were established, at Brick House, Burslem, in 1657.

William Adams 1745-1805
Greengates, Tunstall; was employed by Josiah Wedgwood until 1789 when he established his own factory. Marks impressed: ADAMS; ADAMS & CO; W. ADAMS & CO.

William Adams 1748-1831
Brick House, Burslem and Cobridge, Staffordshire; a great-grandson of John Adams. He founded Cobridge Hall and became a specialist in blue transfer-printed cream coloured earthenware. No marks found.

William Adams 1772-1829
Stoke-upon-Trent, Staffordshire; established in 1790 and made blue transfer-printed ware. His mark ADAMS was impressed or printed. His blue printed ware exported to the United States was impressed with an eagle and printed with the name of the subject in a cartouche.

William Adams 1795-1865
Greenfield, Staffordshire; made similar wares to the previous William from 1820 — also pottery decorated with painted birds. His marks: W. ADAMS & CO and ADAMS.

John Astbury 1686-1743

Shelton, Staffordshire; John, and later Thomas his son, made various wares in a red clay which was ornamented with stamped and applied reliefs in white clay — which was then covered with a lead glaze. John Astbury introduced calcinated flint into Staffordshire pottery which produced a whiter, closer grained texture. Mark: ASTBURY, impressed or incised.

John Ayliff

The first potter to be granted a patent. This was dated 1635 and covered Panns Tyles, Stone Juggs, Bottles of all sizes, Earthen Wicker Bottles, which are now made only by 'Strangers in Forraigne Partes'.

J. & M. P. Bell 1842-70

Glasgow, Scotland; Established 1842 — made transfer-printed earthenware, bearing printed name or initial marks.

Belle Vue Pottery 1826-41

Hull, Yorkshire; Established in 1802 by James and Jeremiah Smith who went bankrupt in 1806. In 1826 William Bell bought and extended the factory and called it Belle Vue Pottery. Large quantities of his pottery was exported to Germany and Holland — his earthenware was 30 per cent cheaper than the Staffordshire variety. Only a small percentage of Belle Vue pottery was marked, usually impressed or blueprinted BELLVUE POTTERY HULL in a circle around two bells.

Castleford, Yorkshire

Established by David Dunderdale in 1790. He made cream coloured earthenware similar to Leeds but not as highly glazed. Marks: impressed D D CASTLEFORD until 1803, then D D and CO CASTLEFORD or D D & CO CASTLEFORD POTTERY after he had taken John Plowes as partner.

Caughley, Shropshire

Established in 1750 by Ralph Browne of Caughley Hall with John Thursfield as manager. They produced cream coloured earthenware until the factory was enlarged and turned over to porcelain. Marks: SALOPIAN or the initials S or C in blue underglaze.

James and Ralph Clews 1818-34

Cobridge, Staffordshire; In 1819 succeeded Andrew Stevenson as makers of blue and white transfer-printed wares. In 1834 the factory closed and James Clews went to America where he founded another factory. He joined Jabez Voudry and Jacob Lewis and established a pottery at Troy, Indiana, specialising in making Staffordshire blue. Lack of suitable clay made the production of white ware impossible and two years later Clews returned home. Later large deposits of fine quality Kaolin were discovered in Troy. Marks: Impressed CLEWS or CLEWSWARRANTED STAFFORDSHIRE with a crown above.

John Davenport

Longport, Staffordshire; Established in 1793 — making cream earthenware and blue transfer-printed. The early ware was impressed Davenport. After 1860 mainly porcelain was produced. Davenports continued under various managers until 1887. Davenport's earliest work was unmarked. The first mark was DAVENPORT printed in red with three small circles underneath. Also used were DAVENPORT lettered in an arc above an anchor and from 1806, DAVENPORT/LONGPORT/STAFFORDSHIRE printed in red and surmounted by an anchor. After 1830 the anchor changed to a royal crown.

Don Pottery

Swinton, Yorkshire; Made cream coloured earthenware from about 1790. Marks: Impressed or printed in red over the glaze DON POTTERY or GREEN DON POTTERY. In the early 1820s the impressed mark of a lion holding a flag or pennant.

Doulton

In 1815, at the age of 22, John Doulton bought a one-third partnership in a pot-house in Lambeth. This firm now traded as Jones, Watts & Doulton. They made salt-glaze stoneware products such as pitchers, butter pots, jars, bottles for beer and ink, soap dishes, tobacco jars, gallipots or gorges. Their main products were bottles for beer, oil and blacking and jars for pastes. No marks.

In 1820 Mrs Jones left the business and it then became Watts & Doulton and then Doulton & Watts and their wares were then marked — DOULTON & WATTS — with or without Lambeth Pottery. Their business was increasing rapidly and they bought more property and more kilns. One of them was especially made for firing unglazed chimney pots, tiles and garden vases.

John Doulton's son Henry joined the firm as an apprentice in 1835 at the age of 15. He was energetic, inventive and phenomenally successful. In 1841 he made a 300-gallon chemical jar and his father displayed it at the entrance of the pottery with a notice saying it was the largest stoneware vessel in the world. Doulton became interested in terracotta sculpture which became an important part of their factory, but the firm was mostly involved with industrial ceramics.

When John Watts retired in 1853 the firm became Doulton & Co and in 1902, a year after the Company had been given the right to use Royal Doulton for its products, a new mark was used on all decorated Doulton wares. Marks were: 1800-1825 FULHAM POTTERY; 1826-1858 DOULTON AND WATTS, LAMBETH POTTERY, LONDON. On many Doulton pieces there are, additionally, the initials of the individual artists.

Elers Ware

A variety of unglazed red stoneware made in Staffordshire by John Philip and David Elers — between 1693 and the early eighteenth century. They established a pottery at Bradwell Wood, Staffordshire which was run by John Philip whilst their shop in Poultry, London was run by David. They sold a hard red stoneware — especially tea pots. Mark: impressed in countersunk relief with a stag and two square 'Chinese' seal marks.

Glamorgan Pottery, Swansea

Established by Baker, Bevin and Irwin in 1813-14 making earthenware until 1839 — using the printed mark illustrated during that period.

Halifax Pottery

Pule Hill, Bate Hayne, Yorkshire; A kiln was built at Pule Nick by the Halliday family in the mid seventeenth century. As it was a rather exposed place, they moved to Bate Hayne and remained there till the late eighteenth century. They made bowls, platters and beakers which were decorated, on the inside mainly, with trailed slip. No mark was used.

Howcans, Yorkshire

Towards the end of the eighteenth century two of the Halliday brothers left Bate Hayne and started a pottery at Howcans. It was very much a family business. The last Halliday — William — remained there till he died in 1916 and the pottery then closed. They made mostly utilitarian wares, pancheons, stewpots, fire bricks and chimney pots, but also a few ornamental wares including money boxes, frog mugs, cradles and puzzle jugs. No marks known.

Leeds Pottery, Yorkshire

This was one of the chief potteries making cream coloured earthenware. Founded in the late 1750s by the Green Brothers, generally the early products are unmarked. From 1775 the impressed mark LEEDS* POTTERY and from 1800 the name HARTLEY GREEN & CO was added to LEEDS* POTTERY.

Liverpool, Lancashire

From 1660 earthenware was made here in quantity and mugs and jugs were made for export. By the second half of the eighteenth century more than 80 master potters were established in Liverpool.

James McIntyre & Co
Burslem, Staffordshire; Made earthenware 1860-1900 — many table and household requirements. Impressed name mark (MACINTYRE) plus monogram mark.

Masons
Lane Delph, Staffordshire; Established in 1797 by Miles Mason at first manufacturing cream coloured earthenware, decorated with enamels. This was called 'Cambrian Argil' from the Welsh clay used. It was impressed with an 'imitation square oriental seal with Miles above and Mason below'. In 1804 Mason was making stone china which he declared was more beautiful and durable than the oriental variety.

Middlesbro' Pottery Co, Yorkshire
Established in 1834 mainly making cream coloured earthenware — mostly domestic. The mark was I.W. & CO. MIDDLESBRO. It closed down in 1887.

Ridgway
In 1792 Job and George Ridgway founded a pottery at the Bell works Shelton, and traded as Ridgway, Smith and Ridgway until 1799 when it became Job and George Ridgway. In 1802 the brothers split up and Job built the Cauldon Place works; Job's two sons joined the company and succeeded their uncle at the Bell works. After Job died in 1813, John and William traded as J & W Ridgway or J. & W. R. or J. W. R. From 1816 they concentrated on the American market and brought out their Beauties of America series — 24 transfer printed views on dinner services. The views were of churches, lunatic asylums, court houses and alms houses in borders of roses and leaves. Another series they did was of Cambridge and Oxford colleges. Their mark was: RIDGWAY.

In 1830 the brothers split up, John had the Cauldon Place works and William the Bell works. William concentrated on the American market and was so successful that he went to America hoping to start a pottery there, but although he selected a site in Kentucky, nothing came of the project. However for the next 10 years he printed a series of American views. John was also very successful and became potter to Queen Victoria and his mark was the Royal Arms with a small JR printed centrally below them.

Rockingham
Established in 1745 by Edward Butler at Swinton near Rotherham, Yorkshire. When he died in 1763 the factory passed through various hands and in 1778 Thomas Bingley and Willoughby Wood acquired the factory and traded as Bingley, Wood & Co. Around 1785 the Swinton Pottery joined Hartley, Greens & Co of the Leeds Pottery and for the next twenty one years the Swindon works were controlled by Leeds, trading as Greens, Bingley & Co at Swinton and Hartley, Greens & Co at Leeds. In 1802 the Swinton Pottery was taken over by John and William Brameld. They were rescued from bankruptcy in 1826 by Earl Fitzwilliam and the works was renamed Rockingham and a griffin — the Earls crest — was included in the trademark. The factory closed in 1842 and the closing down sale notices state:

'*Earthenware* which is very extensive comprehends a general assortment of Table ware including 750 dozens in various patterns of Dishes, Plates, Drainers, Vegetable Dishes, Sauce Tureens, Cheese Trays, Salad Bowls, Bakers etc. 190 sets Chamber Services, Slop Jars, Water Jugs, 400 dozens of Tea Plates, Breakfast Cups and Saucers in great variety; 70 dozens of Tea Plates: 100 dozens of White Bowls, 150 dozens Pints and Mugs; 180 dozens of Jelly Cans, Pressure Jars, Potting Pots, 80 dozens of Sauce Boats, Mustards; 18 dozens of Dahlia Stands; Eye baths; 18 dozens of feeding boats, 17 dozen of Mortars and Pestles, and Paint Slabs, Jugs, Basins etc. and every article for domestic purposes.'

The Rockingham marks were: BRAMELD impressed and, after 1826, a griffin and ROCKINGHAM.

Spode
Stoke on Trent, Staffordshire; Josiah Spode (1733-97) was apprenticed to Thomas Whieldon and when 29 years old he became manager of the firm Turner and Banks; when Turner died in 1770 he acquired the business. He made inexpensive earthenware and sporting jugs and worked on the development of cream coloured earthenware decorated with blue transfer-printing under the glaze. This was perfected and was so successful that in the early 1780s he opened a London warehouse, with William Copeland as manager.

In 1796 William Copeland became a partner in the firm which was now called Spode Son and Copeland. Both men were succeeded by their sons. By 1829 Copeland had become sole owner and the factory went from strength to strength and in 1833 Thomas Garrett became a partner; they traded as Copeland Garrett until 1847. Since then a Copeland has been in control to the present day. Marks: Impressed or blueprinted c1784, Spode or SPODE; from 1790-1820 Spode and a pattern number. From 1805-1820 SPODE'S NEW STONE N.S. was also used, impressed, and from 1805-1833 SPODE in a scroll can be found.

Andrew Stevenson
Cobridge, Staffordshire; The pottery was established in 1808 by Bucknall and Stevenson but four years later Bucknall resigned. Andrew Stevenson became sole owner and concentrated on the American market in which he was highly successful. However his costs were so much higher than most of his competitors that in 1818 his pottery had been acquired by J. & R. Clews. He sent a young Irish artist to sketch American views and 12 of these were put into production and have the artists name stamped in blue. The views, set in scrolls, flowers and wreaths are of New York City, The Battle of Bunker Hill, The Temple of Fame, and New York from Brooklyn Heights. He also produced many English views including Mereworth House, Walsingham Priory, Haughton Hall and Tonbridge Castle. Marks: A crown encircled by A. STEVENSON WARRANTED STAFFORDSHIRE was impressed on all Andrew Stevensons earthenware, or imprinted in blue with the name of the scene accompanied by an eagle, a draped urn or a three-masted ship.

Ralph Stevenson
Cobridge, Staffordshire; Ralph Stevenson was Andrew's brother and he produced blue printed earthenware of outstanding quality. He also produced American views, about 18 in all, with oak leaf and acorn borders, including eight of New York and six of Boston. He also produced English scenes in three groups: Panoramic Scenery, British Lakes and English Views. In the latter group were Harewood House, Oxburgh Hall and Windsor Castle. Mark: STEVENSON impressed.

Joseph Stubbs
Longport, Staffordshire; Joseph Stubbs was another potter who exported to America. His scenes were bordered with flowers, scrolls and eagles, on plates there are three equidistant eagles and there are four on dishes. Amongst his views were those of New York Bay, Hurlgate, East River and Boston State House and Common. Much of Stubbs work is unmarked but his border patterns are used solely by him. A few pieces before 1816 were marked STUBBS, impressed. After that JOSEPH STUBBS LONGPORT in a circle enclosing a star. The impress mark STUBBS AND KENT LONGPORT shows that he was in partnership before he retired in 1829.

S. Tams and Co
Crown Works, Longton, Staffordshire; They produced a series of London buildings design from 1830-50, which included Somerset House, Covent Garden Opera House and the Royal Exchange, all in borders of foliage. Many American views and portraits were also made on foliage borders. They were impressed TAMS & CO, TAMS, TAMS & ANDERSON, TAMS ANDERSON & TAMS. The blue printed ware was also marked with a black stamp with the title of the picture and in the 1840s SEMI CHINA.

Josiah Wedgwood 1730-95
Burslem, Staffordshire; Josiah Wedgwood was the man who, in the eighteenth century, changed the whole course of the European pottery industry. Because Chinese porcelain was so enormously popular in the seventeeth century attempts were made to imitate it. One of the earliest successes was at the Meisen factory and this set the trend for some years. The next to succeed was the Swiss factory and they led the fashion in porcelain for many years. Josiah Wedgwood was first apprenticed to his brother Thomas and then formed a partnership with Thomas Wheildon at Fenton Low in Staffordshire. He began to experiment, devoting his time to improving earthenware. His marks were: WEDGWOOD impressed and WEDGWOOD AND BENTLEY.

Enoch Wood
Burslem, Staffordshire; After the break up of his partnership with Ralph Wood, in 1790, Enoch Wood, backed by James Caldwell, began manufacture of domestic earthenware at Fountain Place, Burslem. He used cathedrals, country seats and castles for his English scenes, such as, York and Durham cathedrals, Warwick and Windsor Castles and Harewood House. The borders were of flowers and vines. The name of the picture is imprinted in a scroll of ribbon. He also did a series of English cities, and London views. The former are marked with an impressed E W & S and imprinted with the name of the view in two scrolls with a bishops mitre and staff. The American views have several different borders, one of the early ones consists of sea shells. In 1820 Wood was commissioned to make a dinner service for a banquet to be held in Boston, in connection with the founding of New England. The border consists of scrolls and four medallions, two with ships and two with inscriptions. He also did Niagara Falls and Lafayette at Washington's tomb. Scenes from the New Testament have scrolls, flowers and motifs from the scriptures round the borders. He also did views of Africa, India, Italy and France.

The early mark was an impressed WOOD with a blue printed trade mark. After 1830 the impressed mark was circular with an eagle in the centre (with a shield), below was written SEMI CHINA and circling all this was E WOOD & SONS BURSLEM WARRANTED. Sometimes there is also a blue-black stamp with the title of the picture, an eagle with a twig in its claws and a scroll coming from its mouth with E PLURIBUS UNUM inscribed.

CONCLUSION

After years of mass-produced goods, whether beautifully made or not, more and more people are turning to individually made articles. Those who are good with their hands get satisfaction, relaxation and pleasure from producing their own work and those who are less proficient but appreciative of individually made items, can buy them at one of the many craft workshops throughout the country.

Cottage industries are flourishing and all manner of crafts are practised, pottery, painting, wood work, wrought ironwork, lace, straw work, candle making, dolls, miniatures, embroidery, glass, leather, weaving, toys and ropework. Everything from bagpipes to miniature furniture for dolls houses.

After World War II, farmers turned increasingly to machines and with the demise of the working horse, blacksmiths with their traditional work diminishing found a second career in wrought ironwork. Gates and lanterns seem to be the most in demand but they will make many other things too.

Small potteries specialising in stone and earthenware abound and the wares they produce are extremely varied. Most of them include kitchenware in their range of goods, in traditional shapes and colours. There are pancheons, bread crocks, salt kits, storage jars, sifters, wine and beer kegs, pie dishes, casseroles, cheese bells and foot warmers, to mention but a few.

Small utilitarian treen utensils are still made and not all of them are mass produced. Rolling pins, butter pats, boards of every shape and size, salt boxes, pepper and salt mills, steak beaters, spoons, bowls and spatulas, all made in a wide variety of woods, can be bought from the cottage craftsmen.

Rural lovers in Wales, unable to carve love tokens themselves for their girl friends, need not worry. Mr Charles Jones of Criccieth still hand carves beautiful traditional Welsh love spoons in oak, beech, yew, holly, apple, pear and cherry.

Of course these crafts that are now so popular — in bygone days a necessity not a hobby — run in cycles subject to the whims and fashions of the day. With the wave of nostalgia for the more leisurely way of life, and the return to the warmth and friendliness of the farmhouse kitchen rather than the severely functional modern kitchen, there is now a tendency to return to the simple products made of natural materials.

Modern Producers of Treen and Earthenware

TREEN

Paul and Margorie Abbatt Ltd, 74 Wigmore Street, London W1: Toys.

Betula Sales Ltd, 27 Ayot Green, Welwyn, Herts: Chopping boards, bread boards, wooden candle holders.

Brown and Waking Ltd, Misbourne Works, Waterside, Chesham, Bucks: Wooden kitchenware.

Michele Esquival and Co Ltd, 35 Friern Barnet Rd, London: Nut crackers, etc.

N. Fisher and Sons (Woodturners), 15 Halswell Road, Clevedon: Loving cups, wassail bowls, wedding cups, birth cups, fertility rattles, lace bobbins, banner poles, and skittles.

Forsetho Crafts, Ross Road, Huntley, Glos: A wide selection of woodware in hard and soft woods. Cheese, bread and chopping boards, salad and sugar bowls in exotic woods, salt and pepper sets. Table lamps, toys and a wide selection of elm garden furniture. Elm refectory tables and chairs, blanket boxes. Tables in yew, elm and walnut.

Dennis French (Woodworker), The Craft Shop, Brimscombe Hill, Stroud, Glos: Bread, cheese, chopping and carving boards, salad and sugar bowls, platters, cruets, toast racks, spoons, scoops, butter dishes and table lamps.

T.H. Godley, 18 Corinium Gate, Cirencester: Salad and fruit bowls, servers, table lamps, tea caddies, cruets, chopping and cheese boards, egg cups and numerous smaller items. Mainly in elm, walnut and yew, with a few less usual timbers.

Charles Jones Woodcarving Workshop, Cricceth, Wales: Welsh Love Spoons.

John Millman, Chippings, Nailsworth Road, Avening: Woodturner, toys, specialising in traditional toys and games.

Douglas Owen (Woodturner), Green View, Marsett, Askrigg, Leyburn, Yorks: A wide range of bowls in various woods, sycamore rolling pins, wooden worry eggs, darning mushrooms, egg cups, pestle and mortars, egg stands, candle sticks and solitaire boards.

Park Green and Co Ltd, Eskdale Rd, The Trading Estate, Uxbridge, Middx: 'Peter Piper' pepper mills and salt mills.

The Peldon Woodturner, Peldon Hall Cottage, Church Road, Peldon, Colchester, Essex: High quality hand turning in English timbers and exotic foreign woods. Salad bowls and servers in elm. Cheese boards, carving boards, hour glasses, gavel and palette, traditional wine goblets, foot stools.

Gus Ravine, 31 Green Lane, Wootton, Northampton, Northants: Goblets, platters, boxes, candle holders, toys and wooden headed rag dolls.

A. Rogers & Sons, Woodware (Chesham) Ltd, 64 Higham Road, Chesham, Bucks: Salad bowls, fruit bowls, steak plates, peppermills, salt shakers, cheese boards, lace bobbins.

I. Schwartz and Son Ltd, 283-9 Cricklewood Broadway, London: Butter curlers and pots.

Karen Wilson, 175 Croydon Road, Caterham, Kent: Welsh love spoons hand carved in traditional designs.

Wilton Ware Turnery, Bishop Wilton, York, Yorkshire: Hand turned wooden lamps, bowls, platters, bread and cheese boards, candle holders in English timbers and teak. Also yew coffee tables and stools.

John R.F. Whitehorn (Woodturner), Green Lane Cottage, Paytoe, Leintwardine, Craven Arms, Salop: All manner of woodturning but specialising in platters, chargers and coasters, boards for cheese, cold meats, cakes etc. Copies made to order of early trenchers and platters. Candlestick maker of ordinary and pricket types.

EARTHENWARE

Aynsley H. and Co Ltd: Earthenware tableware.

Boultons Pottery: Earthenware tableware.

Cauldon Bristol Potteries (Cornwall) Ltd: Earthenware tableware.

Ellgrave Pottery, Burslem, Stoke on Trent: Earthenware teapots and oven to table ware.

S. Fielding and Co Ltd, Devon Pottery, Stoke on Trent: Earthenware — comprehensive range of storage jars and kitchen ware.

T.G. Green Ltd, Church Gresly, Burton on Trent: Stoneware cookware and oven to tableware.

Haverfordwest Pottery, Clay Lane, Haverfordwest, Dyfed: Stoneware — some hand thrown big dishes also honey pots and cast bottles.

Honiton Pottery Ltd, Honiton, Devon: Earthenware oven to tableware.

Hornsea Pottery Co Ltd, Hornsea, Yorks: Storage jars and oven to tableware.

James Kent Ltd, The Old Foley Pottery, Stoke on Trent: Earthenware — plant pot containers, storage jars, tableware, etc.

James Lockett and Co, Middleport Pottery, Burslem, Stoke on Trent: Earthenware hospital ware and apothecary jars.

Mason Cash and Co Ltd, Pool Potteries, Church Gresley, Burton on Trent: Earthenware mixing bowls, pudding basins, pet dishes and cemetery vases.

Masons Ironstone, Hanley, Stoke on Trent: Ironstone domestic tableware.

Geoffrey Maund Pottery, Whytecliffe Rd, Purley, Surrey: Earthenware hand painted kitchen pottery, mugs, tankards, piggy banks, etc.

Moira Pottery Co Ltd, Moira, Burton on Trent: Oven dishes, oven-to-table ware, bulb bowls, pet dishes, footwarmers, bottles, jars.

Stephen Pearce, The Potteries, Whittington Moor, Chesterfield, Derbyshire: Domestic cooking ware, stone bottles, preserving jars, mugs and beakers.

James Sadler and Sons Ltd, Wellington and Central Potteries, Burslem, Staffs: Earthenware teapots, coffee sets, mixing bowls and kitchen equipment.

Spode Ltd, Stoke on Trent: Earthenware domestic tableware.

John Tams Ltd, Longton, Stoke on Trent: Earthenware tableware — beakers, mugs, etc.

Tantallon Ceramics, North Berwick, East Lothian, Scotland: Earthenware storage jars, tiles, coasters, butter dishes, marmalade pots, etc.

Enoch Wedgwood, (Tunstall) Ltd, Tunstall, Stoke on Trent: Earthenware tableware.

Arthur Wood and Son (Longport) Ltd, Longport, Stoke on Trent: Earthenware jugs, bowls, chambers, tankards and vases.

St. Keyne Potteries Ltd, Penhale Grange, St. Cleer, Liskeard, Cornwall.

Tremat Potteries Ltd, Pen Hill Grange, St. Cleer, Liskeard, Cornwall.

Modern Pottery: Old Mill Range by St. Keyne Pottery.

Acknowledgements

The author and publishers acknowledge with gratitude the kindness and help of the following: Birmingham City Museum, in particular Mrs L. Fletcher; Shibden Hall Museum, Halifax, and Miss Norman; Abbey House Museum, Kirkstall, Leeds, Mrs Bridgewater and her super staff; The Castle Museum, York, and Mr Taylor; The Castle Museum, Nottingham, and Miss Wood; My Mother for lending me her Pinto book for so long; my son Adam.

TT
200
.F67

DISCARDED

Forty

Treen and earthenware

ION

HD

a play after Euripides

BLACK SWAN BOOKS

Revised edition

Published by

BLACK SWAN BOOKS LTD.

P. O. Box 327

Redding Ridge, CT 06876

ISBN 0-933806-24-8

CONTENTS

Mr. Bernard Shaw, in his Quintessence of Ibsenism, *writes of a new element brought into modern drama by the Norwegian school. "Ibsen was grim enough in all conscience; no man has said more terrible things; and yet there is not one of Ibsen's characters who is not, in the old phrase, the temple of the Holy Ghost, and who does not move you at moments by the sense of that mystery." Allowing for the great difference of treatment and the comparative absence of detail in the ancient drama, this phrase would, I think, be true of all the great Greek tragedians. In Euripides it is clear enough.*

—Gilbert Murray
Euripides and His Age

ION OF EURIPIDES
1937

For
B. Athens 1920
P. Delphi 1932

People of the Play

Hermes: the god
Ion: a young priest in the temple of Phoibos Apollo
Choros: the queen's waiting-women
Kreousa: queen of Athens
Xouthos: prince regent
An Old Man
A Servant
The Pythian Priestess
Athené: the goddess

Place: *Delphi*   Time: *Dawn*

Translator's Note

CLASSIC GREEK DRAMA *has no division and subdivision of act and scene.*
For convenience, the translator has divided this play into nineteen
sections. These are preceded by explanatory notes. But these notes are
merely the translator's personal interpretation; the play may be read
straight through with no reference, whatever, to them.

These nineteen divisions are sanctioned by the form of the play.
Each one represents an entrance, an exit, a change in inner mood and
external grouping of the characters. For any drama of the strictly classic
or Periclean period, these are few in number. This play is fairly represen-
tative of the proportion; two gods who comment on the beginning and
end; a messenger; in this case, a servant who is also an outside observer,
half-way as it were, between the gods and men; a trinity of father, mother
and son; the father, in this instance, being a divinity, has a double in the
earthly manifestation of the king of Athens; an old man, a stock figure,
and the Pythian priestess who, in the hands of this fifth-century "mod-
ern" genius, is freed from all taint of necromancy and seems also to
predict a type made famous by Siena and Assisi; and last, and not least
important, the choros.

The choros in a Greek play is, in a sense, a manifestation of its
inner mood, expression, as it were, of group-consciousness; subconscious
or superconscious comment on the whole. The strophe and antistrophe
may be spoken by two separate members of the body of the ten or twelve,
leaving the rest to interpret the words, in dance or pantomime, or merely
to serve as formal background for the choros leader or leaders.

The translation is complete, with the exception of: the latter
portion of Ion's monologue, Section VI; Section IX, the greater portion of
the long, polemical discussion of Ion, in reply to the king, urging his
return to Athens; a few lines in Ion's final speech in the same section;
Antistrophe II, in Section XII; and the latter part of the Epilogue, which
is historical narrative, having to do with a prophecy, concerning the
future of the Ionian race.

It is significant that the word ION *has a double meaning. It may be*
translated by the Latin UNUS, *meaning one, or first, and is also the Greek*
word for violet, the sacred flower of Athens.

I

THE SYLLABLES *of these first lines are to be stressed like a gong. They must ring with a certain monotony and assurance. They are the call to attention, the announcement of a curtain about to rise. This curtain is purely imaginary. In fifth-century Greece, the speaker of the prologue enters direct. His entrance is more that of an orchestra-leader than an actor. He is, in fact, that. The quality and timbre of his voice are to set the rhythm of the whole performance.*

PROLOGUE

Hermes

The heaven is held aloft by a giant with
 arms of brass,
Atlas supports the house of the gods and
 the house-roof,
my mother's father; my mother is Maia,
 a goddess;
Hermes speaks, legate of the first of the
 gods, Zeus.

Roughly speaking, there were two types of theatre-goers in ancient Greece, as there are today. Those who are on time and those who are late. The prologue is the argument or libretto; it outlines the plot. The ardent lover of the drama will doubtless be strung up to a fine pitch of intensity and discrimination from the first. The presence of this actor, who impersonates the god Hermes, will actually be that god. Religion and art still go hand in hand. There is, in this country, as we all know, only one word to express its two most sacred abstractions, the good and the beautiful, to kalon.

 We can imagine our enthusiast, as at an opening night of grand opera, being highly disorganized by the whispering of late comers, by the shuffling and readjustment of the audience. We can imagine our dilettante, our casual man-of-the-world, on the other hand, being highly annoyed to find that he has walked in, half-way through the tiresome, reiterated sing-song of the prologue. Then, as now, the character of a theatre-audience was of various degrees of literacy.

Enter the god.

He stands before us; already, we have taken his measure. He will or will not be able to cope with his difficult opening. He might bear a lighted torch. There is no conventional stage property for the speaker of this, or of any Attic prologue. But the torch is symbolical as well as practical. This is Delphi, still night, the sun has not yet risen.

There is no precedent, either, for his carrying a conventionally rolled script. But as writing is under the direct guardianship of this god, it might not be inappropriate. It would be effective if he could place the torch upright on a stand and read the bulky middle part of this prologue, almost chanting it. This would give a rhythmic, hypnotic effect and heighten mystery, in the manner of cathedral litany, heard at the far end of a great vault; our vault, here, is the dome of heaven. All later religious ritual, it might be remembered, is, in one way or another, derived through these earlier presentations. Greek drama was religious in intention, directly allied to the temple ceremonies. Our religious choirs and choruses are the direct descendant of this; a variation of this strophe and antistrophe has been familiar to most of us from childhood, though we may not remotely have guessed its antecedents.

This is Hermes. He has told us that. He is the god of writing, of writers, of orators, of the spoken word. Who could be more fitting as an introducer or announcer? He is the god of wit, of diplomacy, of games; the fleet-feet are, no doubt, bound with sandals. He speaks for his brother, master-musician and prophet, Helios, Phoibos, Apollo, Loxias, king of Delphi.

I have come to Delphi:
at the centre of earth:
where Phoibos chants to men:
priests interpret present and predict future
     events:
there is a town, noted throughout Hellas:
named Athens, for Pallas of the gold-lance:
there, Phoibos loved Kreousa:
daughter of Erekhtheus, on the Acropolis:
masters of Atthis call the place Makra:
that Athenian cliff, great-rocks:
the god kept her father ignorant:

she bore her secret, month by month:
in secret, she brought forth:
she took the infant to the grot:
her bride-chamber:
she left it, exposed as to death:
in the deep basket:
attribute of Erekhtheus, son of earth:
and his descendants:
along with the serpent-necklace:
gift to each true-born Athenian infant:
(because of Athené's first gift:
actual serpents to protect Erekhtheus:
whom daughters of Agraulos nursed):
so a Virgin decked her son for death:
but Helios, my brother, spoke:
go to the earth-born people of Athens:
you know the city of Pallas, you shall take:
out of a hollow rock, a new-born infant:
carry him, his garments and basket:
to Delphi, my prophetic seat:
set him before the entrance of my house:
as to the rest, I will see to it:
for I tell you alone:
this is my son:
I obeyed my brother, Loxias:
I found the reed-basket:
I left the child there, on these steps:
I opened the basket, revealed the contents:
dawn broke:
the prophetess came out:
she saw the child, started back:
what girl (she thought) has left:
a child of pleasure, on these steps:
she was about to cast it out:
but pity prevented that cruel act:
god watched, god wanted:
his child in his temple:

the pythoness brought him up:
she does not know Phoibos is his father:
nor who is his mother:
the boy knows no parents:
the altar gave him bread and life:
a child, he played about its steps:
now the Delphians vote him,
    temple-treasurer:
faithful steward, he is blameless in life:
Kreousa, his mother, married Xouthos:
the Khalkodonidae of Euboia made war on
    Athens:
Xouthos ended that fight:
though no Athenian, he was granted
    Kreousa, as tribute:
he is an Akhaian, son of Aiolos, son of
    Zeus:
long married, he and Kreousa are childless:
therefore they come to consult the Delphic
    oracle:
and Loxias arranges this.

It is necessary to stress the fact that the prologue is by way of being a programme. Or, if we are dealing in musical terms, it is the overture. All the threads of the story are indicated, the plot outlined, the leit-motif *sufficiently stressed. If we are passionate lovers of the drama, we may find this almost the most fascinating part of the play; on the other hand, many a budding Philhellene has struck a snag at the start, decided, on hasty perusal, that Greek drama is out of his depth and has let the whole thing go, after a single dreary attempt to follow the heavy and authoritative opening. Often, sententious platitudes are thrown out to mark time. We must get the audience settled, before we allow the leading actor or one of the almost equally important members of the small cast, to enter. This entrance must not be spoiled; the audience must be keyed-in to the theme, must be in receptive mood, must know roughly the trend of events, so that they may be sufficiently swayed but not over-excited, by certain of the later developments. Of nothing, too much.*

The original speech of the prologue is declaimed without a break. The translator has arranged it in three sections, however, to bring it a little nearer the level of present-day convention.

At Delphi, the enormous stars are still shining. Our prologue stands with his back to the great pillars of the famous temple. The tiers of steps, behind him, seem to mount to infinity. The eyes of the fleet-foot legate of God face us, they face the mountains, above which, a faint glow announces the coming of day. Yet still, the great stars burn in darkness, and still, we ask ourselves what can this all signify; is this a worthy theme for great religious drama, the betrayal and desertion, by one of its most luminous figures, of a woman and her first child? but before the thought actually has time to crystallize, the silver rhythms of this subtle defendant, God's messenger, silence us.

Not meaningless, as you might think,
are the god's plans,
he will give his son to a king,
who will enter this gate,
he will say to Xouthos,
this child is a child of your youth,
so that the boy may go back,
to his mother's house;
his mother shall know him
but the god's act be hid;
the child shall be happy:

not meaningless, as you might think,
are the god's plans,
Asia shall share his fame
and the eastern lands
boast, when they say,
we are called by that name,
Ionians;
this is his wish,
and thus the god speaks,
my son shall be called Ion,
by the men of Greece:

not meaningless, as you might think,
but the time comes
for me to enter the temple,
to hear within,
prophecies of the future;
I turn toward the laurel-gate;
but see—he comes—the son of the god
draws near,
bearing a laurel-branch
to hang on the portal:
now of the gods,
I am first of the gods to speak
a name, famous hereafter,
among men, among gods, among Greeks

ION

II

THE SUN RISES *at Delphi.*

To the acute mind of the fifth-century Hellene this is no miracle. Yet this is the miracle. At this moment, in the heart-beat of world-progress, in the mind of every well-informed Greek—and who of that shifty, analytical, self-critical, experimental race of the city of Athens, at any rate, was not well-informed?—there was a pause (psychic, intellectual), such a phase as we are today experiencing; scientific discovery had just opened up world-vistas, at the same time the very zeal of practical knowledge, geometry, astronomy, geography, was forcing the high-strung intellect on a beat further beyond the intellect. As today, when time values and numerical values are shifting, due to the very excess of our logical deductions, so here. A great English critic has used this play to point out forcibly the irony and rationalism in the mind of the poet. We do not, however, altogether accept his estimates.

Is Euripides ironical, or has his knife-edge mind seen round the edge, round the corner, as the greatest scientists and thinkers of today are doing? Has the circle turned, the serpent again bitten its own tail? This Greek knew that the sun would rise. Yet he hails its coming, as a miracle.

As a student, a thinker, a philosopher, an Athenian, a Greek (only just—at sixty—freed from military service, hence one of the "gerontes"), does this "old man" throw his psyche back into the first lyrical intensities of youth? In spite of the so-called rationalists, and the much-quoted critic with his "irony is lurking at every corner," I prefer to believe that the poet speaks through his boy-priest, Ion, with his own vibrant superabundance of ecstasy before a miracle; the sun rises.

Ion

O, my Lord,
O, my king of the chariot,
O, four-steeds,
O, bright wheel,
O, fair crest
of Parnassus you just touch:
(O, frail stars,
fall,
fall back from his luminous onslaught:)

O, my Lord,
O, my king,
O, bright Helios,
god of fire,
from your altar,
more fire drifts
and smoke
from the incense of sweet-myrrh;

O, my Lord,
from your tripod
the sounds ring,
of the Pythoness
chanting to all Greece,
your commands,
so we greet you,
so we sing;

you are fair,
you are fire,
you are Helios.

Enter priests, from the temple.

You are fair,
you are Delphian
high-priests;
your lips
tuned to his lips,
will soon speak
clear words
to interpret
the magic
oracular
Voice
from the altar;
you will answer
the men here,
who worship;

they are fair;
these high-priests
seek Kastalia,
they will bathe
in that silver, swift
river.

We may relegate the boy, Ion, to the dust-heap and parse his delicate phrases till we end in a mad-house. It will bring us no nearer to the core of Greek beauty. Parse the sun in heaven, distinguish between the taste of mountain air on different levels, feel with your bare foot a rock covered with sea-weed, one covered with sand, one washed and marbled by the tide. You can not learn Greek, only, with a dictionary. You can learn it with your hands and your feet and especially with your lungs.

Taste snow in the air, and distinguish the different qualities and intensities of the wind as it rises from the deep gorge before this temple, or from the drop off the cliffs to the sea, behind it. Realize with some sixth sense, the sea; know that it is there, by the special quality of the shimmering of bay-leaf or some hinted reflex from the sky-dome. Extract from this strophe, one fact; the water is cold in the little river that cuts in a rocky gash, through the other hollow, opposite the temple's sea-side. Does Ion envy these young priests this early-morning, ritualistic libation? We judge so.

Here,
I have other work,
I bind
the sacred wreaths;
I sweep the holy gate,
and with my laurel-branch,
the steps
before the house;
I lave
the marble pavement;
with bow and dart,
I chase
birds

who would mar the gifts;
this was my home
from birth;
this always
was my life;
fatherless,
motherless,
I praise
this sacred place,
the temple
and the god,
Helios.

*Gesture may be simple, direct copy of marble arm and bared limb of
pentellic frieze, or it may tune-in to a less formal era, romantic beat and
barbaric rhythm that have become familiar through the exotic present-day
ballet. There is nothing that cannot be done, choreographically, with
these few stanzas. Ion has a choice of decorative properties; the golden
bow, tall jars or flat bowls and water-pots, the flat gilded wreath or
wreaths bound in the rough, bright natural-green boughs or branches,
ready for trimming and decoration. Ion may even cut and trim these as he
speaks; he moves about with his broom or switch of bound myrtle-twigs.
He may stand, in hieratic posture, scarcely moving, uttering frigid
remote syllables like a marble statue, or he has the whole run and rhythm
of near-eastern colour and exoticism to draw on. He raises his laurel-
branch, as a water-diviner, his rod.*

Strophe   Laurel,
most beautiful,
O, bright
laurel
that sweeps the steps
and the court
of the god Helios;
laurel
gathered within
an immortal laurel-garden,

laurel
cut from a stream
that creeps from a myrtle-thicket
(O, haunted water and blest),
O, laurel,
O, myrtle,
I break
your branch
as the day breaks;
each day
as that avid wing
sweeps blindingly upward,
I bring
fresh laurel
to deck this place;

O, laurel,
O, myrtle,
O, Paian;
O, Paian,
O, laurel,
O, Leto's son;

Antistrophe   let me praise
this spirit,
this home;
let me revere
altar, pillar, rare
tasks I have done;
work can not tire
priests, servants;
immortal joy waits
immortal devotes;

branch sweep
no more,
water-jar
now pour

water,
and gold ewer,
come give
river-water,
hands spray
pure silver,
Kastalia's
crystal water,
lips praise and pray
our father,
no mortal;

O, laurel,
O, myrtle,
O, Paian;
O, Paian,
O, laurel,
O, Leto's son;

Birds flock in here from the high air, above Parnassus. That mountain still towers, unassailable, as in our imagination, the actual temple of the god, though actually its old body, its dead shell lies a heap of battered rocks, its holy-of-holies open to rain and ruin. Long after the actual dæmon was canonically ejected from his immemorial home, a Presence still haunted those weathered stones and spiritually impermeated rocks. So intense and vivid was its power, that those fanatic monks who spared the temple of that sister power, the Virgin of Athens, frantically tore with their own hands at stones, imbued with a Weltgeist *of such inner potency, that its magic threatened even their sincerity. So mighty was the inviolable spirit of this place that those monks, with their utmost fervour, could only dislodge a small number of its blocks, could only break off a small proportion of the images of its façade and of its memorial figures, at turnings of the paved sacred way. So mighty was the reputation of Delphi, that the later apostate, in his dream of a spiritual Greek renaissance, sent ambassadors, in their costliest apparel, with pack animals laden with curious treasures, to hint (subtle bribery) to the meagre body of attendant priests that their day was not yet over. His emissaries, or the Byzantine monarch himself, posed the famous question, "shall the old gods return?" So incontrovertible was its two-edged honour that, even in those days of its imminent decline, that meagre handful of doomed priests preferred Delphic integrity to offers of fantastic power and wealth, and sent back to the emperor Julian at Constantinople, the last message of their oracle, "the new God has risen; the oracle is silent; He has conquered; the water-spring is dried up; the laurel is withered." So powerful, still, was the innate mystery of those forsaken halls, those corridors, that paved sacred way, those altars, that only God himself could break it. A final earthquake sent those mighty walls hurtling down hill, the façade to lie among thistles, the gold to be fouled and tarnished by lizard, snail and the serpent, until brigands finally pried out all the gold that was left, and wandering shepherds, gathering what stone seemed suitable for their mountain huts, left those more fearful broken, marble bits of hands and feet, cursed by man and God alike, to crumble in frost and sun. So incontrovertible is the power of beauty, that within the last century, men of almost superhuman intuition, intellectual devotion and integrity, archæologists of France, have managed to trace wide scattered fragments and re-build, almost in its entirety, the ancient treasure-house of the Athenians at Delphi. Now sharp Ionic columns start up, shafts of unblemished marble point the way to a return; worship the eternal. Indestructible beauty lives.*

So this manuscript of the poet, Euripides, was spared when so much perished; no Savonarola of antiquity or the Middle Ages had power against it. The eagle soars today above the crags of Parnassus. The boy Ion speaks.

Ion	Bird
	of the air,
	O, bright legate,
	wing back,
	back,
	I say,
	to Parnassus;
	off, off the cornice,
	that bright peak,
	that gold ledge
	is no perch for your feet;

O, eagle,
back,
back,
where you hold court,
commanding all birds
with your sharp beak;
back, back to your nest
on Parnassus;

bird
of the lake,
O, fair,
fairest
of birds
and beloved of king Phoibos,
O, swan
of the white wing,
the red feet,
wing back,
back, I say,
to lake Delos;
O, voice that is tuned
to his harp-note,
O, throat
must I pierce you
with my dart?
be off,
O, my swan
lest your blood drip
red death
on this beautiful pavement;

bird
of the wood,
must you have gold?
these gifts
were not set here

for bird-nests;
bird,
bird
of the woods,
seek your forests
by the isthmus
or near
river Alpheus,
my dart
warns you,
here it is dangerous
for you
and your fledgelings;
O, be off;
my arrow has no choice,
nor I;
I am the god's
and I obey;

but
O, you birds
of lake and forest,
you swan,
you wood-bird
and you legate
of Zeus,
even as I string my bow,
I pray,
be off,
be off,
for I must slay
intruders here
within the precinct;

back to Parnassus
and your nests,
back,
back,

O, God's majestic legate,
back,
back,
O, swan,
my Lord's delight,
back,
back,
O, little birds who sing;

for this,
O, this, I would not kill,
your song
that tells to men,
God's will.

III

THE CHOROS *is, as it were, an outside voice, punctuating and stressing moods. It is the play's collective conscience. However, from time to time, speakers of strophe or antistrophe merge, informally, with the actors, or serve to bind contrasting moods. We may imagine that the ladies-in-waiting who enter here, stroll informally, as they might have done in their own city, Athens, through the corridors of this famous temple.*

Personally, I visualize them in blue, one colour of various shades. The strict continuity may be indicated by veils of one shape, but from time to time, as in this instance, it seems to me, the individuality of the members might be stressed. They stand against columns of a temple that may or may not be painted. That stone grandeur was also intensified by primitive bands or upright stripes; black, vermilion, azure, crocus tones are now lost, but they would roughly approximate the effects that the sands and heat of Egypt have baked in, there, for eternity. Certainly, dazzling white features here, as never in Egypt. We may choose our mood, however.

These visitors are intensely interested in the temple. It will be remembered that, in Athens, the Parthenon, on the site of the old shrine but lately destroyed by the Persians, has actually been in a state of construction. Here, we may imagine frescoes painted, in the manner of early Italian primitives. The poet, a painter in youth, is no doubt actually describing art treasures of Delphi itself.

1st semi-choros *Strophe I*	O, Athens, Athens, we revere your god-of-the-beautiful-street; O, Athens, we know how fair are your altars, how white your pillars, but no more fair than this twin-pediment

that reflects the light
of Helios,
child of Leto;

2nd semi-choros   O, Athens,
we know that you are fair,
but here,
what grace,
look where the son of Zeus
strikes at the Lernian pest,
look at this gold,
his knife;

1st semi-choros   Look at this torch; how fair,
Antistrophe I   this cuirass;
is it Iolaos
who helped the son of Zeus?
once,
I embroidered this;

2nd semi-choros   look at this horse
who leaps
upwards with wings,
with this
hero
who slays a beast,
three bodied,
with fiery breath—

1st semi-choros   —and
Strophe II   this—

2nd semi-choros   look at that wall of granite,
the fight of the giants—

1st semi-choros   —here,
there—

2nd semi-choros	—and this who holds aloft the aegis, dragon-wrought, threatening Enkelados; who is it?
1st semi-choros	Pallas, goddess—
2nd semi-choros	—and here fire shoots from the great hand of Zeus—
1st semi-choros	—yes, yes, he kills a giant, Mimas, the hideous; and with his ivy-staff (ivy is meant for peace), Bromios slays a son of earth.

Their delight before the carved and painted treasures of the temple repeat, in minor tone, the rapt intensity of the words of the boy, Ion, who during or before this scene has crept off, perhaps to a distant point of vantage, to stalk another of these foragers, those birds whom he so loves and whom, contradictorily, he must slay. The women see him now. Perhaps they have come across him, in a far corner where they have clustered to examine the last fresco or painting or sculptured group. Or else the boy himself has walked toward them, realizing no casual visitors, but people of importance, whose head-dresses and embroidered robes proclaim them inmates of some great house. He waits without speaking, until one of the women addresses him.

Choros *Antistrophe II*	Hail, you before the temple-gate, we wish to enter, may we pass?
Ion	you may not;
Choros	may we ask a question?
Ion	ask;
Choros	does actually, this inner court guard omphalos, earth's sacred rock?
Ion	yes; garlands deck the sacred place, where Gorgons watch;
Choros	ah, famous spot;
Ion	if you would enter to consult the oracle, you must first make propitiation, special gift of a slain ewe;
Choros	we only want to look about; we would not violate these rites;
Ion	look where you will;

Choros	our lords invited us to visit here;
Ion	what lords? from where?
Choros	Athenian rulers; ah, but there, our lady comes, go, ask of her.

IV

THE QUEEN OF ATHENS *stands before us. How long has she been standing? If the delicate robes of her waiting-women are kingfisher or midnight blue, hers seem to fall in folds that are cut of pure stone, lapis. She has always been standing there. She seems, simply, a temple property that we have, so far, neglected. Her women move, singly or in groups, through the corridors, taking, for all their elegant convention, humanity with them. Kreousa has the inhumanity of a meteor, sunk under the sea.*
    The boy knows this.
    He recognizes it.
    Here is something akin to himself; here is rock, air, wings, loneliness. Who is this?
    We do not know how long they stand, looking at one another.
    The boy at least, is staring at his mother. He realizes, however, with a start, that her eyes are closed. Apparently, she has been standing rapt, gazing at the holy beauty of the temple. But this is not so. Her eyes are fast shut.

Ion

O, beautiful woman,
who are you?
O, rare beauty,
O, grace that proclaims you
a princess,
O, goddess,
what rain
mars that marble,
your face?
eyes shut
in a mask,
see not glory,
nor beauty,
nor this place;
you weep,
while others all rejoice
in this splendour,
the temple
of Loxias.

Kreousa	O, fair, O, strange voice, it is right that you ask why I weep; I looked on this house, I was caught by an ancient regret; I stood here, I was far off, I thought: "you are doomed, race of women, O, woman and women, and lost; why hope and of whom can you hope, whom the Dæmons betray—"
Ion	speak not, O, what torment—
Kreousa	my arrow is gone; who let fly venomed anger, is quiet.

A woman is about to step out of stone, in the manner of a later Rodin. It is impossible, at this moment, not to swing forward into a—to fifth-century Greece—distant future. This poetry rises clean cut today, as it did at the time of its writing. And today, we may again wonder at this method and manner of portraiture, for the abstract welded with human implication, is in its way, ultra-modern.

A woman is about to break out of an abstraction and the effect is terrible. We wish she would go back to our preconceived ideas of what classic characterization should be. It seems this queen of Athens had leapt

forward that odd 450 years that separates this classic age from our own.
She is mother of sorrows, indeed.

Ion	who are you? what city? what name?
Kreousa	Kreousa, an Erekhthian, of Athens.
Ion	O, dweller in a famous place, what parents, what city, what race; I envy, O, I envy you this—
Kreousa	envy this, but naught else—
Ion	is it true, what men say?
Kreousa	is what true? I would know— .
Ion	earth begot, your begettor?
Kreousa	Erekhtheus, yes; can race help?
Ion	freed from earth by Athené?
Kreousa	by her hands, virgin, motherless.

If we knew Greek perfectly and had each one of us the peculiar gift of rhythmic sensitiveness and awareness of tone value of skilled musicians, we might manage to convey in the spoken words something of the emotional tension behind them. Or on the other hand, if we were completely conventionalized mummers in masks, speaking by rote, in a sort of hypnotic sing-song, we might deal with this dialogue in a convincing manner. Or else, if we were standing before an altar, really deeply moved, part of an immense ritualistic ceremony, attuned to audience and the god beyond the altar, we might arrive at some satisfactory emotional solution. What is there left for us?

The broken, exclamatory or evocative vers-libre *which I have chosen to translate the two-line dialogue, throughout the play, is the exact antithesis of the original. Though concentrating and translating sometimes, ten words, with two, I have endeavoured, in no way, to depart from the meaning. The son and mother outline this same story in suave metres. Their manner is that of skilled weavers, throwing and returning the shuttle of contrasting threads. There are just under a hundred of these perfectly matched statements, questions and answers. The original reads as sustained narrative.*

The choros returns towards the end of this dialogue.

Ion　　　　　　　　—yes, in pictures—

Kreousa　　　　　　　—Kekrop's daughters—

Ion　　　　　　　　—had a basket—

Kreousa　　　　　　　—but their neglect—

Ion　　　　　　　　—caused their own death—

Kreousa　　　　　　　—Erekhtheus—

Ion　　　　　　　　—from the great cliff—

Kreousa　　　　　　　—hurled the sisters—

Ion　　　　　　　　—how were you left?

Kreousa	—still an infant—
Ion	then an earthquake—
Kreousa	—blow of trident—
Ion	—slew your father?
Kreousa	O, rock Makra—
Ion	—Pythia claims it—
Kreousa	—evil, evil—
Ion	—dare you say it?
Kreousa	—crime was done there—
Ion	—whose wife are you?
Kreousa	—of a stranger—
Ion	—but a great prince?
Kreousa	—grand-son of Zeus—
Ion	—strange to your rocks?
Kreousa	—near Euboia—
Ion	—sea-waves wash it—
Kreousa	—Xouthos helped us—
Ion	—his sword won you?
Kreousa	—prize of combat—

Ion	—are you alone?
Kreousa	—with my husband—
Ion	—what do you want?
Kreousa	—we ask one thing—
Ion	—wealth or children?
Kreousa	—we are childless—
Ion	—you are childless?
Kreousa	—Phoibos knows it—
Ion	O, my poor heart—
Kreousa	—you, who are you?
Ion	—the god's servant—
Kreousa	—given or sold here?
Ion	I am Loxias'—
Kreousa	—child, your mother?
Ion	I don't know her—
Kreousa	—where is your house?
Ion	—this is my house—
Kreousa	—you have been here—
Ion	—ever since birth—

Kreousa	—who was your nurse?
Ion	I knew no nurse.
Kreousa	O, I weep now—
Ion	Pythia loved me—
Kreousa	—but since grown up?
Ion	—strangers help me—
Kreousa	—but your mother?
Ion	I am, maybe—
Kreousa	—no; what fine stuff—
Ion	—robe of a priest—
Kreousa	—but your parents?
Ion	I have no clue—
Kreousa	—ah, the same hurt—
Ion	—what hurt—tell me—
Kreousa	—I have come here—
Ion	—you have come here?
Kreousa	—for a friend's sake—
Ion	—what does she want?
Kreousa	—I dare not speak—

Ion	—speak and tell me—
Kreousa	—she was Phoibos'—
Ion	—do not say that—
Kreousa	—and had his child—
Ion	—no, a man's act—
Kreousa	—no—it was god—
Ion	—child of Phoibos?
Kreousa	—hid in the rocks—
Ion	—where—where is it?
Kreousa	—she bids me ask—
Ion	—has it perished?
Kreousa	—she thinks, wild beasts—
Ion	—but why think that?
Kreousa	—she looked for it—
Ion	—did she find tracks?
Kreousa	—there was no trace—
Ion	—when was all this?
Kreousa	—how old are you?
Ion	—could god do that?

Kreousa	—her first—her last—
Ion	Phoibos took it?
Kreousa	—if so—alas—
Ion	—is there no hope?
Kreousa	—for you—what hope?
Ion	—for me? don't speak—
Kreousa	—poor child—she asks
Ion	—but one weak point—
Kreousa	—one? all is black—

Ion

will god speak of that
which he would keep hidden?
alas, how dare we ask?

Kreousa

the tripod is given by god
to the whole of Greece,
to answer, what we ask;

Ion

how dare we question the god
and injure his honour?

Kreousa

and of her, of whom we speak,
whom he made suffer?

Ion

Are you mad?
what priest
dare invoke
in his house,
a voice,

to speak judgment
on him,
whom the augurers
worship?
have you lost
all sense of yourself?
do you think
we may challenge the god,
and here, in his very-house?
how barren,
how profitless,
were prophecy,
forced
by the high-priest;
what good were it
to consult
bird-flight
or the slain beast
for auguries,
which the god
forbids?
provoke not
unwilling utterance;
it were useless
and worse than useless;

Choros

many
are the griefs of man,
many,
many,
each different;
many are the sorrows
and strange,
of man,
the unfortunate;

Kreousa

so,
here and in that other place,
you are equally negligent,

so,
holy Phoibos,
you never saved that poor child,
who was yours to protect,
nor now
reply to that woman
(whom,
absent,
I represent),
so that she may seek the tomb,
at least, know
he is no more here,
but a shadow;
so,
holy Phoibos,
why ask further
(for her whom you disown),
of you,
who are god?

but
speak not
of this;
they are back
from the grot
of Trophonius;
Xouthos
would misinterpret
the act of this woman;

O, poor
lost woman
and race of women,
alike;
O, chaste,
O, lawless;
man made your law;
for you all,
there is one
judgment.

V

IN HIS OWN WAY, *this chieftain from a neighbouring province of Greece is a no less impressive person than the queen herself. Probably, in a purely mundane sense, he is more striking. This king may appear alone, from this subsidiary visit to the preliminary oracle, the grot or altar of Trophonius, or accompanied, for the sake of effect, with any number of soldiers, a group of civil attendants or young aristocrats. It may be imagined that he would wear sumptuous garments for this state visit to the oracle. He is inquiring not only for himself, but, as it were, for the whole of Hellas, concerning its future ruler, his heir.*

In the last section, there was a tense feeling of ecstasy and an undercurrent of hysteria, as if the pent emotions of a childless woman and of a motherless boy might, at any moment, break through the surface of hard-won reticence. Here is a counter to all that. The queen's unconscious hatred may stab out at her husband, in vituperative innuendo, nevertheless he stands there, solid, conservative, loyal. He does not even faintly realize her predicament; that is fortunate. If Xouthos had met her, had touched, at all, on her other life, she would not have been able to keep this inner sacred chamber of her spirit, free. She has lived only half a life with him. No doubt, he has guessed this, but his queen will never know it.

Fate has given him a difficult part to play. He plays it with dignity and without imagination.

Xouthos	Hail,
	O, Phoibos;
	may the god
	be honoured first;
	next,
	hail,
	O my queen;
	Am I late?
	you are frightened?
Kreousa	no,
	no;
	only

waiting—
anxious—
tell me
what the oracle says;
do we remain
hopeless?

Xouthos

Trophonius
does not predict,
but says,
"wait the god's utterance;"
nevertheless,
he too spoke;
neither you nor I
shall return
childless.

Kreousa

O,
holiest mother,
perhaps, after all,
our visit
was fortunate,
perhaps, after all,
your son
may be fair
to us;

Xouthos

fair?
but, of course;
where is the god's
prophet?

Ion

I watch
the outer court,
beyond,
nobles of Delphi,
chosen by lot,
guard
the innermost temple;

Xouthos

my thanks;
I am ready
to enter;
I hear,
in fact,
that the oracle
now speaks
within the court,
for all worshippers;
let this holy-day
be propitious;

take
laurel-branches
and wait,
O, queen,
by the altar;
ask there,
that I return from the inner house,
with good news
of the future;

Kreousa
(aside)

ask?
ask?
take laurel?
he has yet a chance,
this One,
to repair hurt;
ask?
ask?
he may yet grant
help;
in any case,
I am powerless;
I cannot accept
the Dæmon,
but I accept
the Voice.

VI

ALL THIS TIME *our Greek sky has been changing.*
Ion carries the laurel-branch, attribute of priesthood, the wand of
power. This branch has been, so far, only the humble instrument of a
boy-sweep before a temple. Nevertheless, we can imagine gestures that
might well command the whole circle of the hours. What time is it?
     Greek unity gives us freedom, it expands and contracts at will, it
is time-in-time and time-out-of-time together, it predicts modern time-
estimates. But the sun, at any rate, has been rising.
     It must be very hot, or there is an expectation of heat, a feeling
toward propitiation, as the boy turns to the water-jars, in order, not only
to cleanse, but to cool the great square stones that lie flat to the blaze of the
Lord of heaven, before the threshold of his very house.

Ion   Why does she talk like this,
              this woman?
              what does she hint?
              she seems to hide something;
              she speaks
              cryptically;
              would she consult
              the Voice
              for herself
              or another?
              in either case,
              she blames Helios;
              but what does it matter?
              Erekhtheus's daughter
              means nothing
              to me;
              Erekhtheus?
              daughter?
              who are these people?
              I'll get on with my work,
              sprinkling water
              from this vase

or this gold jar;
but—

Helios,
answer me;
say
you are blameless;
could you take
a mere child
and betray her?
could you betray her
and leave
your own child
to die?
no,
no,
no,
you are our Lord,
our virtue—

you punish
man's evil;
you could not
(it were unjust),
break laws
made for mortals.

VII

THOUGH THE FUNCTION *of the choros is primarily spiritual, or in a subtle poetical sense, psychological, it has also its very definite useful purpose. Not the least of its utilitarian functions is that of serving for what modern drama means, in its full sense, when it alludes, in one way or another, to the, or to a "curtain." The falling of a curtain, in present-day dramatic art, as we all know, does not simply mean that the room or outdoor scene is shut off. Time is marked, and in subtle ways; even the shortest time indicated may be pregnant with other-idea, other mood or other dramatic pattern. So too, with these women, when they sing or chant or recite words. The words often are complete and logical comment, on the play's progress. Yet sometimes they have no more to do with it than the decorative sign of (say) a historical pageant dropped across an indoor "period" scene to which it has no actual relation in time or space. To the fifth-century Athenian, much of the mythological ornament of the choros is purely decorative.*

On the other hand, this poet had, we have been told, a disconcerting way of shocking the sensibilities of his contemporaries. This antistrophe, for instance, is curiously "human," startlingly personal, after the sonorous appeal of the strophe to chriselephantine beauty and flawless, detached, deified virginity.

Strophe	You who have never known
	the perils of birth,
	you who were born,
	with the help of a giant,
	Prometheus,
	from the forehead
	of Zeus,
	come,
	O, Athené,
	come;
	step down
	from the marble wall,
	from the gold shale
	of Olympos;

come
to the earth-heart,
the tripod,
the temple
of Phoibos;
chant,
O, great Niké,
and you,
Artemis,
sister of Helios,
Virgins both,
pray to the Voice,
pray to the tripod,
the dance;
lest Erekhtheus' race be lost,
grant a child,
O, child
of Leto:

Antistrophe

for what is a man's life
without children?
his court
is flowerless;
his wealth
is a barren gain,
without a child
to enjoy it;
what is a child?
a help
in sorrow;
a joy
in peace;
in war,
our very-heart,
the throb of our heart-beat;
O, give me a child
for delight,

no royal palace;
O, childless,
O, barren wife,
how dead your heart
if you think,
luxury better than this,
a child's touch,
a child's kiss.

Epode

O,
grot
of Pan
and rock
close to the rock of Makra,
you saw three sisters dance;
grass swayed
by the porch of Pallas;
the rocks gave back the notes
of your flute,
O, Pan,
in that place,
where a Virgin
left a child,
her child
and the child of Phoibos;
O, unhappy girl,
she left
her child,
prey of the wild-hawks;

O, tell me,
have you seen,
woven on tapestries,
a happy tale of a child,
born of god and a woman?
have you heard such a tale spoken?

VIII

Sᴛᴀɢᴇ ᴅɪʀᴇᴄᴛɪᴏɴs *for a Greek play must be entirely inferred from the context. We do not know whether the boy has been standing the whole time, sitting thoughtfully on the steps, wandering about with his myrtle-branch or erect in some rapt pose, as he watches the distant sky for the down-flight of some hovering bird, or whether he walked away with the last tragic questioning about the purpose of his divinity. Did he go into the temple to gain spiritual strength? Has he been listening to the choirs inside, the harpists, the lute and flute-players? Has he stood outside the very sacred circle that surrounds the holy-of-holies, the tripod where the high-priestess, the Pythia, gives the strange two-edged answers to those who have come to learn the future, at this famous shrine? Does he himself ponder the wording of a question, which, later, he is on the point of asking: who he is, after all, and how he had got here?*

We can only infer something of all this, let our own imaginations fill out this harmonious outline. We can, if we are strictly of a purist tendency, leave the place bare, imagine the choros in hieratic posture, scarcely moving. Or we can imagine the trail of various priests, officials from the town even, visitors who may cross and re-cross, votaries with presents. The mind has full power of expanding the "romantic" life, in and out of the court, the come and go of worshippers through the great doors. Or, as I say, we may preserve the strictly "classic" outline, the great pillars, the formal tense figures of the chanting women.

Ion

Hail,
you before the temple gate,
O, women,
answer;
where is your master?

and
what does the tripod sing?
what hope
has your king?

Choros   we know not,
he waits within
but there—

the sound of the bolts,
they throw back
the temple-door,

he is here.

IX

IF ONE DEPARTS *from strict ritual, entrance, exit, the upraised palms of prayer, the mystic circle of dance, the stately entrance, at most, of a few priests in the background, one's imagination takes one, perhaps, too far. How far? Music seems to break across, a clash as of muffled cymbals from within the temple, as the great doors swing back and the king, a god-like figure, straight from the inner sanctuary, with the light of a god and the message on his face, steps forth.*

Enter Xouthos. There is no stage-direction necessary, all that is indicated by the words of the poet: "he is here," says the choros of waiting women, but what does that signify? It may be simply a conventional remark, made in answer to a conventional question. It may be an ex-clamation, as the king, born of a son of a son of Zeus, stands in royal robes, his most beautiful ornaments, but lately put on to honour this god, this king of prophecy and music, Apollo. The light of music, song, rejoicing shines from his face. For the moment, he is transformed by joy, into the likeness of the sun-god, not the youth with bow and arrow or the young musician with the strung harp, but an older, mystical son of the King of Heaven: they are after all distantly related, this boy and this man, whose claims for fatherhood are so quickly doubted.

Does Xouthos walk slowly down the great steps? Does he stand and look at the boy, for a long time, before he speaks, or does his voice resound instantly, like a trumpet, from the door-way?

Xouthos	My own—my beloved—
Ion	—own? beloved?
Xouthos	—your hand—your face—
Ion	—madness—
Xouthos	O, I would only touch—
Ion	—not this—the priest's head-dress—

Xouthos	I find you—
Ion	—and this arrow—
Xouthos	—and you, me—
Ion	—my quiver—my bow—
Xouthos	—you attack your own father—
Ion	—never—father—
Xouthos	—it's true—
Ion	—how?
Xouthos	—we are father and son—
Ion	—who says so?
Xouthos	—the god, your protector—
Ion	—with you, the one witness—
Xouthos	I quote the god's utterance—
Ion	—you mis-read a riddle—
Xouthos	—did I misinterpret?
Ion	—what was his exact speech?
Xouthos	—the first one that I met—
Ion	—you met—where?
Xouthos	—coming out of the temple—

Ion	—yes—should be—
Xouthos	—my son—
Ion	—your own or adopted?
Xouthos	—adopted, but my own—
Ion	—I was first?
Xouthos	—no one else—
Ion	O, strange fate—
Xouthos	—for me, strange—
Ion	—yet—my mother?
Xouthos	I don't know her—
Ion	—does the god know?
Xouthos	I did not ask—
Ion	—am I earth-born?
Xouthos	—earth-born?
Ion	—how am I your son?
Xouthos	—the god said so—
Ion	O—no more—
Xouthos	—my child, as you wish—
Ion	—yet—some affair—

Xouthos	—youth—youth—
Ion	—before you wed?
Xouthos	—never since—
Ion	—and *that's* my nobility—
Xouthos	—your age is about right—
Ion	—how did I get here?
Xouthos	I don't know—
Ion	—from far or near?
Xouthos	I can't say—
Ion	—had you ever stayed here?
Xouthos	—for the mysteries of Bakkhos—
Ion	—alone?
Xouthos	—with a partner—
Ion	—where? whom? what?
Xouthos	—with a Mainad—
Ion	—and you?
Xouthos	—had drunk of the wine-cup—
Ion	—so—
Xouthos	—child, it is fate—

Ion	—but how did I get here?
Xouthos	—perhaps left by that girl—
Ion	—escaped—for this—
Xouthos	O, speak to your father—
Ion	—it is the god's wish—
Xouthos	—at last, you are wise—
Ion	—what more could I ask?
Xouthos	—you do see, at last—
Ion	—a descendant of Zeus—
Xouthos	—it is fate—fate—
Ion	—hail; you gave me life—
Xouthos	—you obey god—
Ion	—my father—
Xouthos	—ah, sweet word—
Ion	—well met—
Xouthos	I am happy.
Ion	But O, my mother, whoever you are, will I never see your face? I want that more than ever;

are you dead,
mother?

Choros   I felicitate
this house,
nevertheless,
I could wish
that the queen
were not childless,
and the race
of Erekhtheus.

Xouthos   O, my child,
the god
has directed things
on your behalf;
we have met;
your natural desire
is mine,
to find your mother;
there is time for that;
leave this place,
come with me,
you shall share
my sceptre
in Athens;
do not fear,
you are rich,
of noble blood;
you are silent?
why do you look
like this?
your face turns
from joy
to despair;

Ion   things seen far off

and near,
are different;
indeed, I felicitate fate
since I have found you,
father;
but listen;
I think
the Athenians,
that earth-born race,
will hate me,
an outsider,
illegitimate,
how fight against it?
if I attain prominence,
I shall be despised;
I shall be despised,
if I do not;

Choros

well said;
may you bring happiness
to her
whom we love most:

Xouthos

but enough
of worry and talk;
can't you be happy?
the moment
I heard of this,
I commanded
a banquet sét
in a festive place,
for a guest;
O, I would celebrate
a birth-day,
my son's,
at last;
O, guest of honour,

rejoice,
you return
to your father's house.

Ion   I come;
but, father,
forgive me
and my soul
that asks:

where is she,
that woman,
my mother?

X

AGAIN *the choros. This time, no decorative expression, pattern of mood simply to mark time, or rhythmic merging of one value with another. They breathe bitter and fiery words as if to prophesy the unconscious reaction of their queen. They feel as one, as a proud, deserted woman might feel.*

Having, as it were, expressed the inner fire and concentrated bitterness of the queen, they perform again their function of "curtain." They indicate time passed and a not inconsiderable space of time, by the fact that the boy and his father are well advanced on the long and difficult journey up toward the heights of Parnassus.

The few words of the epode inflame our imagination. We see a mighty procession, sacrificers, other priestly attendants, a whole company of servants, carpenters, musicians, wine-servants, and last and not least, the delicately stepping donkeys with flagons wrapped in vine-leaves and the bulky jars strung aside their backs. Other animals, too, the asses, goats, the sacrificial rams or bulls, strung, unquestionably, with coloured wool fillets and decorative garlands.

Choros	Tears, tears
Strophe	wild grief,
	pity,
	pity my mistress;
	O, what will our lady
	think,
	when she sees her husband
	and asks,
	"who is this,
	this beautiful youth?
	what is it
	the prophet grants?
	a child to his house;
	I am left
	deserted
	and childless;"

who is this child?
who left
this waif
on the temple-steps?
O, oracle,
you are dark,
you are hiding
a mystery,
there is danger lurking,
a trap;
these are not happy portents;
do you feel it?
this child is cursed:

Antistrophe   shall we speak?
shall we tell her this?
she gave her entire life
to this man who betrays
her trust;
old age
will find her hopeless,
while he will have joy;
in his heart,
he will hate her;
her loneliness
will remind him
of how he stole,
nameless,
into her house
to usurp
her noble name;
O death,
death strike;
may his gifts be despised of the gods,
may his altar-fires die out.

Epode   They are there,

they are there
on the height;
already they reach the peak
and the crag
of the rock, Parnassus;
they are there,
aloft,
in the high air,
where wild Bakkhos
carries the torch,
where Bacchantes
dance in the night;
God grant
that this boy perish;
God grant
that he die in his youth;

these strangers
have stolen our house
and the house
of the old King,
Erekhtheus.

XI

THE QUEEN RETURNS, *in perhaps the most notable section of the drama, with an old man, one of those arch-types of classic art, a Job in dignity, antiquity itself, Saturn hobbling with a long staff; half-blind wisdom doomed to outlive its generation; he must be very old. We learn from the conversation that he was a teacher of the father of Kreousa.*

Perhaps the figure of the noble woman, as she appears with the old man, is the most striking of all her characterizations. In her abstract power, she seems now the very embodiment of that Virgin Mother of her city, Athené, strength, power, wisdom with the abstraction of Time, the grandfather, as it were, of her own brain-birth.

Curious words, these. How can we believe that 500 B.C. and A.D. 500 (or our own problematical present) are separated by an insurmountable chasm? The schism of before and after Christ, vanishes. The new modernity can not parody the wisdom of all-time with its before and after. The poet Euripides, one of that glorious trio of Athens' great dramatic period—the world's greatest—predicts the figure of the new worldwoman; tenderness and gallantry merge in this Kreousa, who yearns in neurotic abandon for a child she has lost, yet at the same time retains a perfectly abstract sense of justice, of judgment toward the highest aesthetic religious symbol of the then known world. She questions the god, and she questions him with emotional fervour and with intellect. Her personality, her unity was violated by this god, by inspiration. She has accepted her defeat, yet has retained her integrity. At the moment of her entrance, she still believes in the justice of the old ideal.

Kreousa   Come with me,
                venerable and dear
                teacher of my father,
                come
                to this altar;
                we will rejoice together;
                Loxias will grant my wish;
                how can it be other?
                it is so sweet to have you here,

kind friend,
old teacher,
I love you,
(though I am your queen)
father;

Old Man

your words
are like your father's words,
noble,
ancestral;
you honour all the old ways,
earth-born daughter;
lead,
lead me to the portal;
stones hurt;
I am so old;
the way is steep
to the temple;

Kreousa

follow me;
look—

Old Man

my spirit flies,
not my feet—

Kreousa

here is your stick;
follow these rocks—

Old Man

my stick is as blind
as I—

Kreousa

my dear,
don't fall—

Old Man

are we almost
there?

Kreousa	here, stand my women; speak, friends of my loom and distaff; what does fate grant? what hope have we of that child for which we ask? speak; for good news, good gifts—
Choros	Daimon—
Kreousa	what?
Choros	alas—
Old Man	what is this, what unhappiness?
Choros	what do we hope but death?
Kreousa	why this— this plaint?
Choros	shall we speak or be silent?
Kreousa	speak— the worst—
Choros	I speak twice-death;

you may never press
that child
in your arms,
O, queen—

Kreousa   aye,
               death—

Old Man   dearest—

Kreousa   I am struck,
               hurt,
               slain—

Old Man   we are lost—

Kreousa   O, my heart—
               my heart—

Old Man   grieve not—

Kreousa   O, grief—

Old Man   let us learn—

Kreousa   learn? what?

Old Man   whether your husband,
               likewise
               is desolate—

Choros   O, old man,
               Loxias
               has given him,
               and him alone,
               a son—

Kreousa	what? this is the end—
Old Man	now living, or yet to come?
Choros	I have seen him, full-grown—
Kreousa	impossible— speak—
Old Man	what did it say, the Voice, (speak clearly) whose is this infant?
Choros	the youth he first met, as he came from the sacred gate, god gave him, for his son;
Kreousa	my palace is empty alas, and I am alone—
Old Man	whom did he meet? speak, speak; where did they meet and when?
Choros	O, lady, you saw the one who swept the temple? that is his son.

Kreousa	God grant

Kreousa
God grant
that I disappear
into thin air,
God grant
that I be carried far,
far out of Hellas,
God grant
that I fall
where the western stars fall,
that I may no more
suffer.

Old Man
what is his name?
do you know?

Choros
he is called Ion,
first-met;

Old Man
his mother?

Choros
we don't know;
we only know
how that father
has gone off
with his son
for a sacrifice;
they prepare
a banquet
in the sacred tent,
to celebrate
the son's return
home;

Old Man
I weep with you,
queen,
this is theft
and an insult;

we are bereft
of the house
of Erekhtheus;

Choros

I weep with you,
queen,
share your exile
and death.

Kreousa

Soul,
soul,
speak;
nay, soul, O, my soul,
be silent;
how can you name an act
of shame,
an illicit act?
soul,
soul,
be silent;
nay, nay, O, my soul,
speak;
what can stop you,
what can prevent?
is not your husband traitorous?
he has stolen your hope
and your house;
all hope of a child is lost;
great Zeus,
O, great Zeus,
be my witness;
O, goddess
who haunts my rocks,
by Tritonis
your holy lake,
be witness;
O, witness and help,
O, stars,
O, star-throne of Zeus;

I have hidden too long
this truth,
I must lighten my heart
of this secret;
I must be rid of it.

O, eyes,
eyes weep,
O, heart,
heart break,
you fell in a trap of men,
you were snared in a god's net;
(are gods or are men more base?)

O, eyes,
eyes weep,
O, heart,
O, my heart
cry out
against him of the seven-strung lyre,
against him of the singing voice;
yes,
to you, you, you
I shout,
harmony, rhythm, delight
of the Muses,
you I accuse;
you, born of Leto,
you bright
traitor within the light;

why did you seek me out,
brilliant, with gold hair? vibrant,
you seized my wrists,
while the flowers fell from my lap,
the gold and the pale-gold crocus,
while you fulfilled your wish;
what did it help, my shout

of mother,
mother?
no help
came to me
in the rocks;
O, mother,
O, white hands caught;
O, mother,
O, gold flowers lost;

O, terror,
O, hopeless loss,
O, evil union,
O, fate;
where is he whom you begot?
(for fear of my mother,
I left
that child
on those bride-rocks;)

O, eyes,
eyes weep,
but that god will not relent,
who thought of the harp-note
while his child was done to death
by hovering eagles or hawks;
O, heart,
heart break,
but your heart will never break,
who sit apart
and speak
prophecies;
I will speak
to you on your golden throne,
you devil
at earth-heart,
your golden tripod
is cursed;

O, evil lover,
you grant
my husband who owes you naught,
his child to inherit my house,
while my child
and your child
is lost;
our son was torn by beaks
of ravaging birds,
he was caught
out of the little robes
I wrapped him in,
and lost;

O, terror,
O, hopelessness,
O, evil union,
O, fate,
I left him there on the rocks,
alone
in a lonely place,
be witness,
O, Delos,
and hate,
hate him, O, you laurel-branch,
hate,
hate him
you palm-branch,
caught
with the leaves of the laurel to bless
that other so-holy birth,
yours,
Leto's child
with Zeus;

heart,
heart weep,

soul,
O, my soul,
cry out,
harmony, rhythm, delight
of the Muses,
you, I accuse
who pluck from the soulless frame of the
    harp,
the soul of the harp.

Choros   Terrible,
terrible
heart-break;
we, too, weep.

Old Man   I am beside myself;
let me look,
let me look at your face;
your words
leave you breathless;
O, breathless,
they follow
in such haste;
I am done,
I am drowned;
O, my daughter,
evil follows
evil; disaster,
disaster;

what is it?
do you accuse
Loxias?
whose is this child
you lost?
where is that haunt
of wild beasts?

O, repeat,
repeat this—

Kreousa   I am ashamed,
yet speak—

Old Man   let me grieve
with your grief.

Again we have another of these long dialogues, to which no translation can do justice. There are roughly another hundred lines, of perfectly matched lyrical conversation; question and answer follow each other in the strictest rhythm and infallible regard to rule of metre and rhetoric; musically, this is the unquestioned classic method of a Bach or Haydn.
    Dramatically?
    We are back again with our old bag of tricks, we are re-working a pattern in a tapestry, we have heard all this before. The dialogue, at times, seems to play almost the same rôle as the prologue; the words may be monotonously chanted, when dramatic sequence allows; they may numb us into some state of affable acceptance; we need some sort of antidote to this high-pitched hysteria of perhaps the most ultra-modern of all this poet's lyric fragments.
    The old man, as Fate's prompter, suggests a melodramatic solution to the predicament. Just kill your husband. The queen of Athens will not do this.
    Kill the boy, then.
    She agrees to this with suspicious alacrity.
    She has loved this boy. She recognized psychic affinity at the first moment of their meeting. Her husband has been given a son by this Voice, that betrayed her in her girlhood. If the son had been any other than just that tall, curious, detached young foundling, to whom she had first spoken in the courtyard of the temple, she could have endured it; or if some other god, Bakkhos or even Zeus had oracularly given her husband that gift. She has been betrayed by God and man alike. Is the logic so flimsy? Is the psychological reasoning so weak? The much-quoted critic speaks of this woman as being a "savage" at heart. This is not the gesture of a frenzied, over-balanced woman. Kreousa retains, at the last her un-

questionable authority. *She is the nearest, in actual descent, to the divinity of the Acropolis; her earth ancestor was born out of these very stones, Athené lifted him up in her hands. That goddess was her foster-mother, her intellectual progenitor. Kreousa, the woman, has failed, now let Kreousa, the queen, speak.*

"I connive at this plot. I, as your regent, give you full authority to strike at the enemy of my house."

She hands the old man the magic poison that was the mystical gift of the very goddess, to her race. She will save its authority, even if her city Athens and all Attica is doomed to die with her.

Kreousa, the queen, stands shoulder to shoulder with the sword-bearer of the Acropolis. She, too, holds a weapon; she, too, strikes infallibly at the enemy of her city. Kreousa, the queen, standing shoulder to shoulder with Pallas Athené, becomes Kreousa, the goddess. The price? Kreousa, the woman.

Kreousa	—you know long-rocks?
Old Man	—you mean Pan's grot?
Kreousa	—yes; there I met—
Old Man	—speak; my heart breaks—
Kreousa	—fearful—alas—
Old Man	—yes, yes; I guess—
Kreousa	I must speak out—
Old Man	—sad, O sad secret—
Kreousa	—but now, no secret—
Old Man	—how did you hide it?
Kreousa	—wait; let me speak—

Old Man	—who helped with this?
Kreousa	—I had no help—
Old Man	—but where—where is it?
Kreousa	—the child? ah, wild beasts—
Old Man	—but the god saved it?
Kreousa	—the god? no—
Old Man	—who left the child?
Kreousa	—who? I—black night—
Old Man	—and who knew of it?
Kreousa	O, no one knew—
Old Man	—but you—how could you?
Kreousa	—how? my heart broke—
Old Man	—O, god's cruel heart—
Kreousa	—his small hands reached—
Old Man	—seeking your breast—
Kreousa	—seeking my breast—
Old Man	—what did you think?
Kreousa	—think? God will help—
Old Man	—alas, Erekhtheus—

Kreousa	—veil not your face—
Old Man	—your father's face—
Kreousa	—fate, fate—fate—fate—
Old Man	—weep not—weep not—
Kreousa	—but what is left?
Old Man	—revenge; strike—
Kreousa	—strike at the god?
Old Man	—burn this, his house—
Kreousa	—that will not help—
Old Man	—your husband, then—
Kreousa	—my bridegroom, no—
Old Man	—then, kill this child—
Kreousa	—what? ah—
Old Man	—a sword will serve—
Kreousa	I go—
Old Man	—on to the tent—
Kreousa	—but—no—
Old Man	—your courage fails?
Kreousa	—secret and sure—

Old Man	—what do you mean?
Kreousa	—from fight of giants—
Old Man	—yes, what of that?
Kreousa	—sprang monster Gorgo—
Old Man	—to fight the gods—
Kreousa	—but Pallas slew it—
Old Man	—that frightful form—
Kreousa	—those writhing serpents—
Old Man	—I've heard of it—
Kreousa	—Athené's aegis—
Old Man	—she wears the shield—
Kreousa	—among the gods—
Old Man	—but what of this?
Kreousa	—you know Erekhtheus?
Old Man	—your ancestor—
Kreousa	—Athené gave this—
Old Man	—yes, yes, speak clear—
Kreousa	—to him, a talisman—
Old Man	—and of what nature?

Kreousa	—blood-drops of magic—
Old Man	—strung on a necklace—
Kreousa	—in a gold amulet—
Old Man	—your father had it—
Kreousa	—and now, I have it—
Old Man	—how does it work?
Kreousa	—one blood-drop heals—
Old Man	—the other?
Kreousa	—slays—
Old Man	—are both together?
Kreousa	—can good and bad mix?
Old Man	—safe, safe at last—
Kreousa	—with the boy's death—
Old Man	O, let me help—
Kreousa	—when we get back—
Old Man	—no; here were best—
Kreousa	—in Athens, true—
Old Man	—you will be suspect—
Kreousa	—a step-mother—

Old Man	—accused of murder—
Kreousa	—yes, yes, yes, yes—
Old Man	—none shall guess this.

Kreousa

Take this amulet,
it is ancient
Athenian gold-work;
look for that secret place
where my husband
makes sacrifice;
there,
at the end of the feast,
as they lift
the libation-cup,
pour this,
(hidden
beneath your cloak)
into the boy's goblet;
but only into the one
of that would-be lord of my home;
one drop
and it is done;
and he shall never see Athens,
nor Athens see
that false son:

Old Man

and you,
go back to the town;
I'll see that all is done;
O, old, old feet,
you are strong;
what is age?
I shall strike again
a blow,
at those who have wronged

my lords;
I was old in my time
and wise;
but now,
now,
now
I am young.

XII

AGAIN *the choros marks time for us. We may imagine them now in their most abstract mood; their dark scarves drawn tight, they are the dark or sombre hours; they call upon the witch-woman who dwells at cross-roads, she who guides the murderer's hand, the instigator of hidden magic. This is good old classic melodrama. Nothing is spared us. Let the blood of the dragon in the magic filtre slay this youth, for if he lives, our mistress will not. She will hang herself, she will plunge a dagger into her heart and so on.*

As I say, the choros is the march-past of hours, their time-values are ultra-modern, accordion-pleated, as it were. They may minimize the passage of time, or in a few stark words, they may convey an impression of hours lapsed. Here, we are made to realize the actual setting of the doomed feast. And the choros of witch-women, now taking tone from their queen, the leader of their moods and emotions, reviles the sun-god. Who is he, anyway? No such things, we can imagine them thinking, ever happen in our holy city. There, intellect, justice, integrity rule, and gods and men step forth to prescribed formula. This sun-god had mixed the vibrations, has committed that most dire of spiritual sins, he has played fast and loose with the dimension of time and space. He appeared for a whim, to a girl, and that girl, their queen; and, for a whim, deserted her. A god should know his place, all values have been reversed. And does this pretender, this waif, know what it's all about? And now the poet himself forgets this threnody in his sheer delight of words; they again seduce him, as it were, in spite of himself—or in spite of these doleful hours—into a by-play of vibrant images, dance, sea-floor, stars, a gold crown, a Virgin.

This poet's golden images seep up, inevitably; they are like treasure seen far, far down under black, sweeping storm-waves.

Choros	Demeter's
Strophe I	daughter,
	mistress of cross-ways,
	Hecate,
	step forth;
	yourself,
	yourself

mix the cup,
preside
at the feast of death;
fill the goblet,
with blood-drops
of the earth-born
dragon,
(in that tent,
as our queen directs),
for him
who would steal our house;
for no stranger may pass
our gate,
as a king,
none rule
but a child
of Erekhtheus;

Antistrophe I   for this is the end
of us all,
if the plot fail,
the end of our queen;
she will pierce,
with a sword,
a vein;
she will knot
a cord,
a halter
about her throat;
she will seek life
in another place;
not here;
this sun-light shall not fall
on an outcast,
an alien,
thrust
from her own door;

Strophe II   too much is said of this god,
too much is sung,
too much of the sacred spring;
what of deeds in the night?
will that boy ever know?
will he see what the torch-flame saw?

will he watch the stars on high,
the moon and the moon-dance?
will he wonder?
will he witness
the sea-dance,
fifty Neriads,
in and out
of the sea-wave,
on the sea-floor?

will he worship,
adore
the Virgin,
gold-crowned,
and the holy Mother?

this waif,
from a temple,
would steal,
betray,
take
the throne
of another.

XIII

THE DISHEVELLED *forward-rush of a servant tells us what we already know, what we have known for a long time. Kreousa's plot must fail. Here is another time-worn device of classic drama, this servant is the familiar Messenger, who shares with the prologue, as a rule, the honour of holding the stage longest. The Messenger is to the end, or the middle-end of the drama, what the prologue is to the beginning. Infallibly, he picks up threads that have already been woven and re-woven, finds loose ends, unravels here and there and re-weaves, till there can be no possible loose-stitch, no blur in the out-line, no rough seam, no hint of clumsy handiwork. Indeed, the Attic drama was fitly presided over, by that patron alike of all subtle spinners and thinkers, Pallas Athené.*

Servant	Women, where is your mistress, daughter of Erekhtheus? I have looked here, there, everywhere in the town;
Choros	what— what is it, O slave? what do you want?
Servant	they're after her— she's to be flung from the precipice—
Choros	speak— (have we been found out?)
Servant	I heard that— yes, you're in it—
Choros	but the plot— who discovered it?

Servant	the god; does he rank evil above justice? it was his act—
Choros	yes, yes, but quick, tell us, do we live? is life our fate? or death? do we die?
Servant	They left the temple, they came: to the festive place, where priests: prepared the altar, where burnt: the fire of the god Bakkhos: there, Xouthos rendered thanks: for his son: he stained the rocks: with the victims for Dionysos: the husband of Kreousa spoke: now set the tent upright: I visit the gods of birth: if I am late, invite: the guests, begin the feast: he took the votive beasts: he went; the boy set up: the tent-poles, fastened taut: the cloth, to shield from heat: of noon or the setting-sun; a plethron long, square-shaped: the whole stretched out, firm set: a thousand feet, a room: for the Delphic people's feast: and now he covered it: with the temple-treasure, stuffs:

beautifully wrought with work:
from the Amazons; on the roof:
was the cloth-wing Heracles brought:
as spoil to the house of Phoibos:
Ouranos shone on the cloth:
the sun drove the sun-chariot:
to the west, with the star Hesperus:
the moon, dark-clad, went forth:
with her steeds unyoked; aloft:
stars wheeled; Pleiads, the giant:
with sword-hilt, Orion, and last:
the Bear turned his length round a
    north-pole:
of gold, while Selene shot bright:
rays for each month; and the tempest:
stars, Hyades, gleamed till the luminous:
Dawn drove the stars back:

moreover, he fastened yet:
more beautiful cloth; strange ships:
enemy-oars fight Greeks:
there are men, half-man, half-beast:
and a deer and a wild-lion hunt:
Kekrops with his brood by the entrance:
curved his tail; some Athenian's gift:
and here, in the midst of the tent:
they placed gold kraters; a legate:
stretched to his height, blew a blast:
on the trumpet, to call to the feast:
all Delphi; when all was placed:
they served them, they crowned them, and
    last:
a very old man came up:
to greet them; he made them laugh:
with his curious gestures; he helped:
pour water, he lit sweet-myrrh:
he made himself wine-butler:

with the flutes, he ordered the last:
great, gold-wrought, thanks-giving cups:
he selected the finest goblet:
hail, our new master; he dropped:
poison, (none knew of this) the queen's
    gift:
into the cup; as the youth lifted it up:
in prayer, a servant spoke:
an ill-omened word; as priests':
companion, himself, a priest:
the youth interpreted this:
bring a fresh krater; he spilt:
his wine and invited the guests:
likewise, to empty theirs out:
as libation, unto the earth:
in silence, fresh wine was brought:
mixed Byblos; doves from the gate:
flew in; they are safe in the court:
of the temple; they dipped their beaks:
in the poured-out wine, flung back:
their feathered throats; one dropped:
shuddering, at the youth's feet:
it beat its wings, it wept:
the guests stood up, alas:
it stiffened; its purple feet:
curled under, in death:

who has attempted this? (the boy:
the oracle's choice, flung back his robe:
leapt up); speak, speak, old man:
you sought my death, the cup came from
    your hand:
he caught the old man by the arm:
surprised in the very act:
he confessed the sacrilege, Kreousa:
the amulet; the young priest rushed out:
with the guests, to the place of judgment:

O, sacred earth, be witness:
and you, O, Pythian fathers:
(he spoke to the court) a stranger:
the daughter of Erekhtheus:
has sought my death:
their vote was unanimous:
the lords of Delphi spoke:
she plotted against a priest:
she would have taken his life:
and in the sacred House:
let her be hurled from the rocks:

now the whole town is out:
your mistress came to this place:
to ask from its god, birth:
he commands death.

XIV

A SHORT *lyrical rhapsody, or threnody, from the choros, after the smooth narrative of the Messenger, reminds one of the first appearance of Ion, and his outcry against the birds from Parnassus. We remember how he aimed his arrow, at the same time uttering a prayer for the safety of winged messengers of God. Like an old nordic wood-tale or myth of folk-lore, the bird whom our hero had propitiated in the beginning, in the end, saves him. It is a dove, who, according to divine pattern, offers himself as sacrifice.*

There is a waywardly mystical tone in this classic writer as if he, like his hero-dæmon or god-villain, had mixed time and space, played fast and loose with convention of here-and-now. A later Byzantine writer might have invoked this image of a bird slain for a human-spirit, or the most vibrant of Augustine Latins might have been criticized for being over-ornate with this mixed imagery, taste, sight, colour, a white bird we presume, with its breast stained scarlet. The flock of birds seems intrusion from one of those spice-islands of the great lyric period of Greek poetry— with their voices, we see palm-shadows, the grape itself is not more intoxicating to our senses than, to our sight, the sway and delicate fluttering, as they group around the wine-pool. On my visit to Delphi, I was surprised to find coral-branches of our so-called Judas-tree, cutting irregular, jagged purple against the weathered masonry of ruined porches. Here is the same shock, as of an intrusion, against lined marble and stark Doric column, of the most exotic of eastern patterns; fragrance, colour, taste—as if the poet had, inadvertently, spilled wine-purple through the pure line-ing of his own verse.

Choros

Now is there nothing left;
for us, it is manifest,
hers
is our death;
a dove was the cause of it;
with the sweet of the vine,
he tasted
the blood-drop
of death;

alas,
my life;
alas,
my mistress;
she shall be hurled
from Parnassus;
would I had wings
and could fly;
would I could creep
through the earth;
they will stone me
to death;

O, for a chariot,
O, for a ship—
escape;
can a god help?
O, most unhappy
mistress,
what is your punishment?
there is one law,
one judgment;
he who plans ill
for another,
must himself,
suffer it.

XV

ACCORDING *to immemorial Greek law, a fugitive may take shelter at the altar of the god. Especially was this so at Delphi, high court of justice, both political and ecclesiastical. We may still run our fingers over stones, read with our spirit a sort of immortal Braille, that informs us of this and that slave, purchased back from his master, with his own earnings, or escaped or given to the god, presented with his own freedom, in other words, as a token of love and trust, by a former owner. Because of this immemorial tradition of the right of the fugitive, the attendant ladies of the queen urge her, on her frantic, hunted entrance, to take shelter by the altar. In this two-edged Delphi there was civil law—but over and beyond it was, definitely, a law we too often arrogantly claim as peculiar to our own times, the law of mercy.*

Kreousa	I must die, I am caught, they condemn me to death—
Choros	we know, O unhappy woman, alas—
Kreousa	I escaped the town, but what use? I am lost—
Choros	the altar—
Kreousa	can that help?
Choros	a suppliant— you are safe—
Kreousa	but the law decrees —death

Choros	the god's law protects—
Kreousa	they come— see—their spears—
Choros	but quick, mount the step, stand there by the altar; if fate will, you escape, he who strikes, will be banished.

XVI

Iᴏɴ *had accepted second-best and he knew it. Nevertheless, the mortal youth was intoxicated with a sudden insight into mundanity. His foster-father was a wealthy and distinguished soldier, of a renowned family, not an Athenian, to be sure, but for all that, a stalwart member of the old aristocracy. The boy who had yearned all his life for the mere come and go of ordinary people, of ordinary human contacts, was suddenly over-whelmed by this brilliant festival. The sacrifice, at its inception, to the god, was by way of a decorative convention, part of the banquet, not really savouring of those old ritual ceremonies, in the temple, that had lain all those brilliant hours far, far down below in the valley, at his feet. He had climbed high, in a moment; and what is this mere legal question anyhow, of parentage worth, we can imagine him asking himself, as the procession of musicians and court-entertainers pass before him. It is conceivable that Xouthos had brought with him his personal body-guard from Athens, and the formality of their acceptance of the adopted son of their chief must have been overwhelming. His head has been turned in a moment.*

Was he not, at heart, the son of that luxury-loving, yet totally vibrant and detached musician? Did Ion not feel, at last, that the old ritual was out-worn and those priests and pythonesses of his childhood, antique mummers and old dolls? Here was life, living.

In a moment, it was to be swept from him.

At the exact second, as his hand reached out, and his material body was to be sworn-in as it were, to a brotherhood of mastery and battle, the hand drops.

There is a greater brotherhood.

He does not yet know this.

He only sees a woman cowering by an altar. Her veil is torn. Who is she? Of course; the change is startling but that is what she was like, always. The image of the tragic, stark-eyed queen whom he had first met in this very courtyard, has shrunk. She is, after all, only another failure. Perhaps his own soul, still recognizing their actual spirit affinity, for that reason, the more reviled her. He too, in a moment, would be dragged back into this psychic hinterland of loss, doubt, loss of personal identity, loss of mundanity, loss of material position, that terrible groping depersonaliza-tion of all true sons of the sun-god, music, and inspiration.

He shouts at her, in anger; he drags out invective. His manner is over-done. It is necessary to over-compensate, over-stress, over-act his part. For it is only a part he is acting, and he, unconsciously, must know it.

But Kreousa, on the other hand, has found something that all the time was there. In spite of invective against her lover, in spite of the recurrent motif of loss and desertion, in spite of the reiteration, the accusing tirade, was she too, like her own son, arguing down something in her own spirit, rather than inveighing against mere outside circumstance? It seems now, we guess for the first time, that the spark lit by her lordly lover had never really gone out. She clings to the laurel-branches on the altar and she clearly gets the better of her son, in this argument: what is the god to you? *he asks. She says,* my body is his by right, *and even more significantly,* I am safe with the god.

Would Kreousa of Athens, virgin and queen, at last analysis, have chosen a lesser lover than the lord of light?

Ion

O face of a monster,
what dragon begot you?
what devil,
what flame?
your evil is worse
than that Gorgon
whose blood-drop
was your weapon:

catch her;
she shall lie at the base
of the mountain,
Parnassus;
her hair
shall be torn
on its crags;

my good Dæmon was near me,
it heard me,
it saved me

from this,
a step-mother
and strangers,
the insult of Athenians;
away from my friends,
I had entered her trap;
she had done me to death;

and now do you think
that the altar will save you,
the laurel, the temple?

you weep?
tears are due
my own mother
(I never forget her)
not you;

look how she shakes,
trick upon trick,
no prayer
shall avail you.

Kreousa   I am safe with the god;

Ion   what is the god to you?

Kreousa   my body is his, by right;

Ion   who would have killed his priest;

Kreousa   you are your father's, not his;

Ion   I was always his near-son;

Kreousa   you were—but my day has come;

Ion   you are his in crime, I, in beauty;

Kreousa	I fought the enemy of my own city;
Ion	I came, didn't I, with a mighty army?
Kreousa	you did, to destroy the house of Erekhtheus;
Ion	—what flame, what torch?
Kreousa	—dishonesty, theft—
Ion	—my father's gift—
Kreousa	—*his*—the city of Pallas?
Ion	—his sword saved it—
Kreousa	—he never owned it—
Ion	—you feared my future—
Kreousa	—your death or my death—
Ion	—you envy my father—
Kreousa	—you steal from the childless—
Ion	—my father's property—
Kreousa	—a sword, a spear—
Ion	—let go the altar—
Kreousa	—so? find your own mother—
Ion	—you'll pay for this—

Kreousa	—on the altar-step?
Ion	why should you wish to die mid the laurel-wreaths?
Kreousa	so I may grieve One who brought me grief;
Ion	this is preposterous; O, it is not right that evil should crouch in this marble, holy place; only the saintliest hands should touch the laurel; only the priests, by right, should mount this stair; away, away with her—

XVII

BUT THIS *is too much. The boy-priest, that detached spirit, who in the opening scene of this drama had been invoking pure-spirit in the heaven and praying for the very lives of those whom he was forced to slay, is crying out against that most ancient and remotely sacred of all religious institutions, that unquestioning right of the fugitive, king or beggar, slave or general, to ask, if luck grants him the will to get there, help, with the last gasp of his earthly body, of the inviolable altar of justice-beyond-justice. Luck or the god had willed that this queen find foot-hold on the rim of the altar, strength to climb that stair, breath to cry out her right to the indubitable protection of the divinity. And this youth, formerly so remote, so holy, so removed from all evil contact, his whole life one hymn of praise to the deity, must thwart her. He may question the right of the sun to rise by day and the stars by night but not the right of the fugitive to demand pity of the god. This right is immemorial and immemorial votaries guard it. Such a one, steps forth.*

"I am the Pythian priestess," she says. The boy falls back. There is no higher title, not one more honoured, in the whole civilized world. "I have been honoured of Phoibos, and I speak."

She is not young, this woman. It was against the veils of her early novitiate that those small hands had clung. The frozen body of the deserted waif was warmed before the brazier, burning in the inner-temple. His feet and hands were laved with holy water. And by whom? By the Pythoness of Delphi.

No slight honour for a mortal; even if he had been that, these ministrations would have conferred immortality upon him. Ion can struggle no longer with the fate that proffers him divinity. He bows his head, "mother," he says, "of my spirit."

The Pythia	No;
	peace;
	I,
	prophetess,
	honoured of Phoibos,
	first among all the women of Delphi,

chosen
to protect
the temple's
ancient rites,

I,
even I
left the tripod,
stand here,
speak:

Ion   mother of my spirit:

Pythia   mother; the name is sweet:

Ion   you have heard of this woman's plot?

Pythia   I have, but are you blameless?

Ion   I struck at a murderess:

Pythia   she was wounded, a stricken wife:

Ion   more—a vengeful step-mother

Pythia   no: my son, leave this place:

Ion   how? what have I in life?

Pythia   Athens; go with pure heart:

Ion   to strike at evil, is pure:

Pythia   you must know why you strike:

Ion   was I wrong? are you right?

Pythia   look at this old box:

Ion	a basket, with faded fillets:
Pythia	you were left here in this:
Ion	what? impossible—speak—
Pythia	I reveal things, long secret:
Ion	but why have you hidden this?
Pythia	it was the god's wish:
Ion	and now, what does he ask?
Pythia	having found your father, depart:
Ion	who told you to keep the basket?
Pythia	the Voice spoke to my spirit:
Ion	and asked what? what?
Pythia	that the basket be given back:
Ion	for what good or what evil purpose?
Pythia	all your little things are here:
Ion	to help me to find my mother?
Pythia	when god wills, not before:
Ion	O, day, O, too luminous:
Pythia	take this; search carefully for her; do everything yourself,

neglect no spot
in Asia,
search all Europe
for your mother;
I love you;
it is the god's wish,
dear child,
that I give you back
this:
(O, how carefully
I have kept it);

I do not know why
the god asks this;
no one in the whole world
knew I had it,
nor where I hid the box;

hail;
I have loved you
as much as any mother,
yet
you must find her;
first, ask here;
some Delphic girl
might have
left her child
on these steps;
ask of the Greeks;

this is my last command
(the god speaks
through me),
farewell.

XVIII

SHE HAS GONE, *that most beautiful wraith, that ghost from antiquity, and the boy's uneven duality must cry out in agony as he seeks to find the balance between the detached introversion of the temple servant and the dream of easy mundanity, power and human delight. There is a third Ion to be born from the struggle of these two, the Ion whose power is predicted by the speaker of the prologue, a spirit yet a man, the founder of distant colonies, the protector and progenitor of Greek culture throughout Asia and the world. From Ion the spirit and Ion the mortal, is born a third, compound of man and god, Ion, the Ionian.*

But this birth, like all birth, is physically painful, and spiritually heart-breaking.

He holds a painted box in his lap, bound with old cords, faded fillets or ribbons.

Like a child with a box of toys from one dead, his head falls forward on the painted lid.

Ion, the Ionian, will be born of this box, but the youth in painful state of transition, now asks, who am I? After all, this parade on the hill-top may turn out to be the most humiliating and ironical of farces. I may be the child of the meanest slave in the lowest quarter of the outer town of Delphi or even from some malsain *village, further along the sea-coast, he thinks. Then he opens the box.*

Ion

And now,
I weep;
think;
my own mother
(secret bride)
hid me in this very box;
I never touched her breast;

I am nameless;
I really lived a slave's life
in this place:

true,
the god,

always was exquisite;
the rest?
bad luck;

O, all those years
lost;
mother—

how she must have suffered;

O, my cradle,
I offer you to the god,
(although I am yet ignorant,
as to whether I am a slave's son;
perhaps it will be worse
to find that mother,
than not);

Helios,
I consecrate this
in your precinct;
what shall I do next?
I must do what he asks;
I must look inside it;
I must open the basket;
I dare not fight
fate;

O, sacred fillets,
why were you kept
from me?
O, cords
round the basket,
what have you hidden?

how fair,
this basket,
so carefully kept—
for what?

Kreousa	you—you—there—
Ion	O, quiet—away—do not touch—
Kreousa	no, no, no, give it back; it's my child's basket—
Ion	she is mad, catch her—
Kreousa	kill me rather— I don't care; I will have it, and all the little things in it— my basket—
Ion	she is terrible with her lies—
Kreousa	no; thank you, thank you, too, you've helped— you, you dear—
Ion	dear? but just now, you wanted to kill—
Kreousa	I didn't know, I didn't know you—

Ion	tricks, more tricks—
Kreousa	I can prove—
Ion	and I; what's in this basket?
Kreousa	your little dresses—
Ion	very well, but what?
Kreousa	O, I can't speak—
Ion	speak; you seem to know—
Kreousa	there's a blanket, my own embroidery—
Ion	what's on it?
Kreousa	I didn't even finish it—
Ion	well, what's the pattern?
Kreousa	I began a Gorgon, in the middle—
Ion	God—
Kreousa	then, there're serpents round it, like an aegis—

Ion	yes, here it is—
Kreousa	O, childhood task—
Ion	what else?
Kreousa	dragons of gold-work—
Ion	the charm of Athené—
Kreousa	in memory of Erekhtheus—
Ion	what are they for?
Kreousa	a sort of necklace—
Ion	it's here— but there's one thing more—
Kreousa	yes, there's one thing more;

O, olive
of Athens,
O, crown of wild-olives,
I plucked
from the very holy rock;
it is sacred;
the very branch,
the goddess herself
brought;

it never loses its silver
immortal
leaf;
it is there;

Ion   mother,
my mother,
most dear—

Kreousa   son,
O, light,
more lovely than Helios
(and the god will pardon this),
you are in my arms
at last,
I had thought you lost,
long ago,
with the ghosts
in death—

Ion   alive
and dead,
both—

Kreousa   Io;
what cry is there,
what joy from the lips
can answer
the joy in my heart?
Io;
speed joy
through the luminous
high air:

Ion   this has happened
more swiftly
than thought—

Kreousa	I tremble still with terror—
Ion	did you ever dream of this?
Kreousa	dream? where is the prophetess? I would ask who brought you here—
Ion	be happy, why ask? it was the god's wish—
Kreousa	how did I bring you forth? O, tears— how did I let you go? I breathe at last—
Ion	I, too—
Kreousa	mine is no barren house; Erekhtheus puts forth a branch and flowers; the earth-born race again sees light; O, light, Helios—
Ion	my father must know of this—
Kreousa	your father?
Ion	why not?

Kreousa	you had another father—
Ion	alas—
Kreousa	hymen which gave you life, had no torch-procession, no chant—
Ion	I am ill-begot—
Kreousa	let Pallas speak—
Ion	what?
Kreousa	ah, she who sits on my rocks, she knows, Pallas of the olive-branch—
Ion	speak out—
Kreousa	on the Acropolis, haunted of nightingales, Phoibos—
Ion	why Phoibos?
Kreousa	I was his bride—
Ion	fate— speak—
Kreousa	I had (in the tenth month)

the secret child—
of Helios—

Ion if true—
how sweet—

Kreousa only a girl,
a mother,
I wrapped him up
in this—
look, I embroidered it—
and you—
why, it was you—
you never touched my breast—
I couldn't even wash
your little feet,
I left you alone in the desert
for foraging hawks
and death—

Ion how could you?

Kreousa I was mad,
I might have killed you—

Ion and I might have
murdered
you—

Kreousa it's over,
don't speak of it—

Choros let no man despair
after this—

Ion but mother,
I hate to speak,

but—
tell me the truth;
O, tell me,
I'll understand;
you loved secretly,
were afraid,
said a god—

Kreousa   no,
by Athené Niké,
by Victory
and her chariot,
by her battle for Zeus
against giants,
I swear:
no mortal was your father,
only this king,
your protector,
Loxias—

Ion   why did he give
away
his son
to Xouthos?

Kreousa   he entrusted you
to a king,
as a man may make his friend,
his child's
guardian—

Ion   I doubt—

Kreousa   stop;
you dare not doubt;
Helios wanted you
to reign in a noble house;

he can not give you your birth-right,
his name,
as father;
O, don't you see?
even I,
even I,
overwrought,
wanted to kill you;
it was he
who watched over you—

Ion

no;
this is impossible;
I'll go to the temple,
I'll ask the oracle,
whether I am a god's son
or a mortal—

but
look—
there on the roof,
by the pinnacle,
hide your face,
hide your face,
mother,
it's dangerous—

a Presence
descends,
there,
there,
a Dæmon;

O, God,
O, Goddess,
O, face,
like the face
of Helios.

XIX

Aɴᴅ ʟᴀsᴛ *but not least,* deus ex machina *steps forth; intellect, mind, silver but shining with so luminous a splendour that the boy starts back, confusing this emanation of pure-spirit with that other, his spirit-father, her actual brother of Olympos. "Flee not," says Pallas Athené, "you flee no enemy in me," and this most beautiful abstraction of antiquity and of all time, pleas for the great force of the under-mind or the unconscious that so often, on the point of blazing upward into the glory of in-spirational creative thought, flares, by a sudden law of compensation, down, making for tragedy, disharmony, disruption, disintegration, but in the end, O, in the end, if we have patience to wait, she says, if we have penetration and faith and the desire actually to follow all those hidden subterranean forces, how great is our reward. "You flee no enemy in me, but one friendly to you," says the shining intellect, standing full armed, in a silver that looks gold in the beams, as we may now picture them, of the actual sun, setting over the crags and pinnacles of Parnassus, shedding its subdued glow upon this group, these warm people who yet remain abstraction; a woman, her son; the haunting memory of a wraith-like priestess; the old, old man; the worldly king and general; the choros, so singularly a unit yet breaking occasionally apart, like dancers, to show individual, human Athenian women of the period, to merge once more into a closed circle of abstract joy or sorrow; the boy again in his manifold guises; the woman who is queen and almost goddess, who now in her joy wishes to be nothing but the mother of Ion; the mother, if she but knew it, of a new culture, of an æsthetic drive and concentrated spiritual force, not to be reckoned with, in terms of any then known values; hardly, even today, to be estimated at its true worth. For this new culture was content, as no culture had been before, or has since been, frankly with one and but one supreme quality, perfection. Beyond that, below it and before it, there was nothing. The human mind dehumanized itself, in much the same way (if we may imagine group-consciousness so at work) in which shell-fish may work outward to patterns of exquisite variety and unity. The conscious mind of man had achieved kinship with unconscious forces of most subtle definition. Columns wrought with delicate fluting, whorls of capitals, folds of marble garment, the heel of an athlete or the curls of a god or hero, the head-band of a high-priest or a goddess, the elbow-joint of* an archer or the lifted knee of one of the horses of the dioscuri, no matter how dissimilar, had yet one fundamental inner force that framed them, projected them, as (we repeat) a certain genus of deep-sea fish may project its shell. Shell, indeed, left high and dry when the black tide of late Rome and the Middle Ages had drawn far, far out, dragging man and man's æsthetic effort with it. A scattered handful of these creatures or creations is enough to mark, for all time, that high-water mark of human achievement, the welding of strength and delicacy, the valiant yet totally unselfconscious withdrawal of the personality of the artist, who traced on marble, for all time, that thing never to be repeated, faintly to be imitated, at its highest, in the Italian quattrocento, that thing and that thing alone that we mean, when we say, Ionian.

Let not our hearts break before the beauty of Pallas Athené. No; she makes all things possible for us. The human mind today pleads for all; nothing is misplaced that in the end may be illuminated by the inner fire of abstract understanding; hate, love, degradation, humiliation, all, all may be examined, given due proportion and dismissed finally, in the light of the mind's vision. Today, again at a turning-point in the history of the world, the mind stands, to plead, to condone, to explain, to clarify, to illuminate; and, in the name of our magnificent heritage of that Hellenic past, each one of us is responsible to that abstract reality; silver and unattainable yet always present, that spirit again stands holding the balance between the past and the future. What now will we make of it?

And how will we approach it? Not merely through subtle and exquisite preoccupations with shells of its luminous housing; no. Long ago, an olive-tree sprang up. It was sheltered by the Erechtheum. It was worshipped by virgin choros, procession of children, boys and girls; by the older girls; by the wise men of the city; by the heroes about to depart for Marathon; by poet and sculptor, king and visiting prelate. The Persian swept down on the city. We all know of this. We know how not one stone was left upon another, how the old wooden temple that held the ancient dragon and the smiling, ironical, thin and fragile goddess herself, striking it back, fell charred, and buried beneath it, other priceless images, a thin Dioskouros mounting to a horse, a weathered Hermes, a Victory, a stone owl, a plaque, inscribed with legal matter, dating from the days of Solon. The mighty olive-tree had been planted by the very hands of the goddess; it was this gift to men that the gods had placed above the *inestimable offering of Poseidon's white, swift horses. The olive was beautiful and useful, it fed and gave that oil, prized alike for food, for anointing Pythian or Isthmian victor, and for ritualistic sacrifice. The charred stump of the tree stood out now among the ruins of the Acropolis. "When our olive-tree dies," the Athenians had been taught from child-hood, "our city is lost." Ah lost—lost city!*

Tradition has it that one devote scrambled back. He was dis-obedient to the injunction of his goddess, blatantly for this one time, rebellious. Of nothing, too much. Of one thing too much, and for the last time, that one thing (we may imagine his tense thought, valiant above his broken heart-beats) beauty. Not the beauty of the lyre-note plucked at dawn, not the beauty of ecstasy of the red-wine cup and song among the dancers, not the beauty of the virgin-huntress knee-deep in wild lilies, not the beauty of the cloudy outline (God of men, of gods) your father, O Athené, resting on the hill-tops; not snow, nor cloud, nor thunder, nor wind, nor rain, nor the concrete projected reality of stone coping nor architrave, but the beauty of pure thought—and he would fall here—his ankles burnt with smouldering beams from the little, painted ark-temple; his torn sandals were scorched, his heart beating, his last heart-beat. O yes, he can remember them, his friends in the little, lost city. They are strapping their miserable bundles, trying to fasten overcrowded or almost empty boxes, ready to flee the Persian, the Persian—lost—we can share his thought, feel the vibration of his rebellion, of nothing too much— *save of this thing. Our love for our lost city.*

There was a new war plague that year with a new name, but his lungs and his knees have come this far to defy her injunction (with his last breath) of nothing too much. *And there by the charred stump of the old, of the immemorial olive, we may hear his last cry.* Of this thing, too much—

Did he sleep, our rebellious Athenian? What dawn saw him rise? How was he wakened? By cold wind, no doubt, from the sea, that blue sea that, always its traditional enemy, had now deserted Athens for good. Poseidon had won at last. He might easily have sunk the straits in white foam, or better, summoned an earthquake to fling up rock bulwarks against the invading splendour of those purple galleys. The sea did not listen to the propitiatory prayers of the holy denizens of his city. He sent no storm to wreck the enemies of Greece—and yet he, too, was Greek.

Faithless and treacherous at the last, he seemed even to encourage with tender sea-breeze the freightage of these robbers. And what had the west to give them that the east had not? Laden with gold and packed with their beaten goblets, the galleys of Xerxes sought wealth here (O, little, ark-like, painted temple of wisdom!) worth all their fabulous trappings, harness for a million stallion, tent-poles of gold, awnings fringed with silver, gold-pricked tapestries. From Athens' ancient enemy, the sea, the dawn came.

Our Athenian's face was black with ashes, so that what he saw was, no doubt, part of the dishevelled humour of his dreaming. He reached out his frozen hand toward the charred stump of the once sacred olive-tree, to find—

Close to the root of the blackened, ancient stump, a frail silver shoot was clearly discernible, chiselled as it were, against that blackened wood; incredibly frail, incredibly silver, it reached toward the light. Pallas Athené, then, was not dead. Her spirit spoke quietly, a very simple message.

How did he get back to his people? What did he say when he finally overtook them, perhaps on the old, sacred Eleusinian highway? What was their answer to the rapture of his so simple, so spiritual message, that told his companions of that hope (from which sprang a later Parthenon). Our old tree is not dead. The Persian has not killed it.

Today? Yesterday? Greek time is like all Greek miracles. Years gain no permanence nor impermanence by a line of curious numbers; numerically 1920, 1922 and again (each time, spring) 1932, we touched the stem of a frail sapling, an olive-tree, growing against the egg-shell marble walls of the Erechtheum.

While one Ionic column stands, stark white and pure on the earth, that name shall live, the power of the goddess shall not have passed, the beauty and the cruelty of her brother shall not be relegated as sheer dæmonism or paganism (whatever, God help us, that word has come to mean), while one Ionic column lives to tell of the greatest æsthetic miracle of all-time, welding of beauty and strength, the absolute achievement of physical perfection by the spirit of man, before the world sank into the darkness of late Rome and the Middle Ages, this goddess lives.

Flee not,

in me
you flee no enemy,
but one friendly to you,
Pallas.

Athené

Flee not,
in me
you flee no enemy,
but one friendly to you,
Pallas;
I come from Athens
in my chariot;
I am sent
by Helios
who fears your reproach;
that is past;

I speak
for Helios;

he is your father;
he gave you to another
so that you might enter
a noble house;
but fearing
(once found out)
that your mother

might slay you,
or you slay your mother,
he sent me;

he would keep this secret;
the Athenians must not know;

but for you,
I fastened my steeds

to my chariot,
for you,
I came
to reveal
mystery;

Kreousa,
go home;
place your own child
on his
and on your throne.

Ion

Pallas,
great daughter of Zeus,
how could one question
you?
how could one doubt
your speech?
what was impossible before,
is clear;
I am the son
of Loxias;

Kreousa

now you must listen,
I speak,
I praise
whom I blamed,
Helios;
he has repaid
my loss;
O, doors,
O, oracular gates,
you were black before,
now
what light,
what light
breaks;

O, handle,
I touch you,
I kiss you,
O, holy door;

Athené the gods' pace moves slow,
do they forget?
no;
blessed be the man
who waits
(nor doubts)
for the end
of the intricate
plan.

Kreousa O, child,
come home—

Athené lead on,
I follow—

Ion what friends,
what a road—

Kreousa lead
to Athens—

Athené and a throne—

Ion for me,

ION

Choros Apollo,
son of Zeus,
son of Leto,

hail,
hail,
O, Apollo;

and you, too,
praise the gods,
that your heart may be free
and your home;

if you love the gods,
you too,
shall be loved of fate;

but you evil
doubter,
you shall be
desolate.

AFTERWORD: *Dawn Drove the Stars Back*

H. D. ATTEMPTED two verse dramas based on Greek themes: *Hippolytus Temporizes* (1927) and *Ion* (1937). Both can be considered as "freely adapted" from plays by Euripides—the latter play being closer to a direct translation; albeit such "translation," in the hands of H. D., becomes (in the words of George Steiner) "inevitably a metamorphic act of interpretation." H. D.'s Greek dramas constitute a "commentary in action" on a Euripidean base, and resemble in this regard the Oedipus plays of W. B. Yeats and Ezra Pound's *Women of Trachis*. In one aspect, all of these are *translations;* in the root sense, a "carrying over" into not only another idiom, but another imaginative framework—filtered through defined artistic sensibilities and transformed into personal symbols.

Euripides was an emblem for H. D.: "Euripides is a white rose, lyric, feminine, a spirit" ("Notes on Thought and Vision"). Before *Hippolytus Temporizes,* H. D. had tried her hand at "straight translation" of choruses from two Euripidean dramas: *Iphigenia in Aulis* and *Hippolytus* (published together in a volume in "The Poets' Translation Series" [1919]) as well as beginning work on *Ion.* And between then and the completion of *Ion,* she translated choruses from two more Euripides plays: *Bacchae* and *Hecuba* (published in *Red Roses for Bronze* [1931]). Referring to her two early choric translations, T. S. Eliot (in "Euripides and Professor Murray" [1920]) found H. D.'s rendering poetically superior. Eliot cited H. D.'s *condensation*—that quintessential modernist principle. And Douglas Bush, while not altogether approving of H. D.'s translations, praised her "salience, energy, and speed"; but he concluded that H. D.'s "translations produced almost exactly the same effect as many of H. D.'s original poems, and if there is one thing certain in the realm of poetry, it is that Euripides was not like H. D."

Hippolytus Temporizes does not claim to be a "translation," even though the plot is based on Euripides' play. Rather the plot elements are freely reworked into a symbolic pattern reflective of H. D.'s own preoccupations, dealing with themes previously depicted in numerous poems and to appear again in her Greek novel, *Hedylus* (1928). While *Ion* is more directly a translation, it also takes its place within H. D.'s imaginative canon—not only through her choice of play to translate—but through the explicit transformation enacted by her interspersed passages of prose commentary inserted directly within the text of the play.

H. D. approached the translation of Greek literature as an intimately subjective experience. In *Bid Me to Live*, H. D.'s surrogate is described in the act of translating:

> She brooded over each word, as if to hatch it. Then she tried to forget each word, for "translations" enough existed and she was no scholar. She did not want to "know" Greek in that sense. She was like one blind who knows an inner light, a reality that the outer eye cannot grasp. She was arrogant and she was intrinsically humble before this discovery. Her own.
>
> Anyone can translate the meaning of the word. She wanted the shape, the feel of it, the character of it, as if it had been freshly minted. She felt that the old manner of approach was as toward hoarded treasure, but treasure that had passed through too many hands, had been too carefully assessed by the grammarians. She wanted to coin new words.

The translator of Greek is envisioned as an inspired intuitive diviner, seeking to "make it new." In *Ion*, H. D. writes of the direct sense experience needed to recreate the fresh Greek feeling for life:

> Parse the sun in heaven, distinguish between the taste of mountain air on different levels, feel with your bare foot a rock covered with sea-weed, one covered with sand, one washed and marbled by the tide. You cannot learn Greek, only, with a dictionary. You can learn it with your hands and your feet and especially with your lungs.

The more obvious aspect of H. D.'s divergence from the Greek form of Euripides is in her handling of the metric lines—at times pared down to one stark word alone, repeated over and over and over again. This, of course, creates H. D.'s own effect: the reiteration indicative of a stunned, traumatic shock; an inability or refusal to absorb what is being said; an hypnotic, trance-like stammering, induced by an overwhelming experience. In place of regular meter and smoothly flowing dialogue (*hypotaxis*), H. D.'s interchanges are *staccato*, jagged and disjointed, run-together (*parataxis*). H. D. commented:

> The broken, exclamatory or evocative *vers-libre* which I have chosen to translate the two-line dialogue, throughout the play, is the exact antithesis of the original. Though concentrating and translating sometimes, ten words, with two, I have endeavoured, in no way, to depart from the meaning. There are just under a hundred of these perfectly matched statements, questions and answers. The original runs as sustained narrative.

H. D. dismantled the blocks of continuous narrative into fragments of intercolliding retorts, forming a type of *stichomythia*. The rhythm defined by such meters is modernist—similar to that employed in music by Igor Stravinsky in *Oedipus Rex* and Carl Orff in *Oedipus der Tyrann* and *Antigonae*. The brusque, vigorous syncopation established by H. D.'s "exclamatory *vers-libre*" intensifies and essentializes. The repetitions become mantric incantations, registering dull thuds of impact, as realization slowly sinks down into the psyche to register; the characters remaining motionless, as held by a magnetic gravity of great density. Truly these plays have been not only *translated* but *transformed* into H. D.'s own idiom and vision. "The music of meaning has altered" (George Steiner).

I

IN HER "Notes on Recent Writing" (June 5, 1950), H. D. stated that her drama *Hippolytus Temporizes* had "for theme and centre, the portrait or projection of the intellectualised, crystalline youth, whose prototype is again found or first found in the actual Greek drama." In the figure of Ion appears the prototypical "crystalline youth." Of unknown parentage, the young man, temple servant to Apollo at Delphi, lives wholly dedicated to the god; his life simplified to the clear contours of a marble statue. The instrument of Ion's life of service—a laurel broom—symbolizes both his present humility and his forthcoming honor. Numerous resemblances exist between Ion and Hippolytus: "the boy-priest, that detached spirit, who . . . had been invoking pure-spirit in the heaven and praying for the very lives of those whom he was forced to slay"; "this youth . . . so remote, so holy, so removed from all evil contact, his life one hymn of praise to the deity." In this instance, the deity is Apollo, god of light, who remains invisible as the background for the drama, while informing the action with an all-pervasive influence. The essential tone of the play is struck repeatedly by Ion: the entire play is a paean to light. *Ion* glows throughout with the aurora of the god's presence.

Set against this lyric, sacramental note of praise stands an accusation: can a god be a betrayer? Voiced by Kreousa, the unknowing mother of Ion, this evidences a seeming contrast between unfeeling gods and suffering mortals. Kreousa has approached Apollo's sanctuary in tears. Is radiant light, sublime but remote, capable of easing her pain? "So may I grieve One / who brought me grief," she asserts. "Are gods or are men more base?"

Upon first appearance, Kreousa stands stone still:

> The Queen of Athens stands before us. How long has she been standing? If the delicate robes of her waiting-women are kingfisher or midnight blue, hers seem to fall in folds that are cut of pure stone, lapis. She has always been standing there. She seems, simply, a temple property that we have, so far, neglected. Her women move, singly or in groups, through the corridors, taking, for all their elegant convention, humanity with them. Kreousa has the in-humanity of a meteor, sunk under the sea.

As in a trance, Kreousa weeps; Ion stares: *stasis*. "Here is rock, air, wings, loneliness"; natural elements and solitude. Gradually, painfully, Kreousa emerges from immobility as a woman arising from rock in a late work of Rodin: "a woman is about to break out of an abstraction." This coming to life—this *emergence*—enacts a pivotal role in the play, both as technique for performance and essential motif. Time and again, H. D. draws attention to the visual patterns created by the performers. The central alternation between stasis and movement reflects the thematic dichotomies: art and life, the divine and the human, the abstract and the emotional. The play's rhythm pulses between these poles.

II

Ion is essentially envisioned by H. D. as a music drama composed of melodic song and gestural dance. Following the opening chant-like monody of Hermes' declamation—producing "a rhythmic, hypnotic effect"—occurs Ion's aria, hailing the sunrise as an ever-recurrent miracle. The play develops into counterpoint with the staccato dialogue retorts exchanged between Ion and Kreousa, gradually attaining resolution in the harmonic unison of the concluding section. H. D. allows for an openness of treatment for the movements of the chorus: "Gesture may be simple, direct copy of marble arm and bared limb of pentellic frieze, or it may tune-in to a less formal era, romantic beat and barbaric rhythm that have become familiar through the exotic present-day ballet." Both a harmonic approach, in which movement and color are subtly blended and modulated (in the manner of Jaques-Dalcroze's or Rudolph Steiner's eurythmy) or one of sharp contrasts and jagged movements (as in Nijinsky and Bakst's *Ballets Russes* productions) are left possible. "There is nothing that cannot be done, choreographically. . . ."

III

SUBLIMINALLY running throughout the play is "a tense feeling of ecstasy and an undercurrent of hysteria," of pent-up emotions which threaten to break up surface composure. The buried reality propels; the hidden emerges—or is projected out of the psyche. The matrix for the distillation of conscious realization is the Unconscious. The play depicts the gradual rising of consciousness—reflected in the sun's course—brought about through blind, mistaken conflict. Ion and Kreousa, even though sharing a psychic affinity, are both in ignorance of Apollo's design. The chorus acts as a "collective conscience," a manifestation of the play's inner mood, "expression, as it were, of group-consciousness, subconscious or superconscious comment on the whole." The chorus constitutes a corporate psyche, ranging from physical perception to heightened awareness. Framed between the night scene of the prologue and the pre-dawn opening of the action and the sun's setting in the concluding section, the progress of consciousness is paralleled by the arc of light. Juxtaposed against the objective and external measurement provided by the sun's course is a relative and fluid time-sense, reflecting the inner situation:

> All this time our Greek sky has been changing. . . . What time is it? Greek unity gives us freedom, it expands and contracts at will, it is time-in-time and time-out-of-time together, it predicts modern time-estimates. But the sun, at any rate, has been rising.

Mother and child, unwittingly united in an identical pursuit, both grope toward self-consciousness. Kreousa possesses secret knowledge which she keeps buried, since it is illicit, based as it was on an experience of the divine. She maintains half of her life—the transcendent—apart: "this inner chamber of her spirit, free." While "her personality, her unity was violated by this god, by inspiration, she . . . accepted her defeat, yet . . . retained her integrity." Kreousa is a divided self; Ion, however, appears all too one-sidedly integral. Yet Ion also is split: "the boy's uneven duality must cry out in agony as he seeks to find the balance between the detached introversion of the temple servant and the dream of easy mundanity." In Ion is also apparent the division between the transcendent and the transient. The task to be accomplished is the attainment of wholeness, based not on a choice between "either/or" but on a conjoining of both dimensions.

IV

THE RECONCILIATION of opposites is brought about in the play through the mediumship of the Pythian priestess. Uniting contrasts—bridging the upper and lower worlds, the super-conscious and the sub-conscious, the realms of gods and men—the Pythia brings the hidden to birth. As oracle, the Pythia, possessed by the god in the form of a serpent, was archaically connected with the underworld and death. However, the Pythia in *Ion* is wholly purged of darkness; "freed from all taint of necromancy," she is rather a type of *duecento* Madonna, "a type made famous by Siena and Assisi." This "wraith-like priestess" should well serve H. D. as an etherealized emblem of the artist. Referring to an entirely different Ion (in this case a fifth-century Athenian rhapsodist), Plato, through the mouth of Socrates, designates the poet as one "possessed, inspired," a "minister of the gods"—linked with diviners and seers: "the poets are nothing but interpreters of the gods, each one possessed by the divinity to whom he is in bondage"; "it is the god himself who speaks, and through them becomes articulate to us." Poets, speaks Socrates, are "not in their senses" but raised in Bacchic transport: "a poet is a light and winged thing, and holy, and never able to compose until he has become inspired, and is beside himself, and reason is no longer in him." ("Ion," trans. Lane Cooper, in Plato, *The Collected Dialogues* [Bollingen Series LXXI])

In uniting the over-mind with the sub-conscious, the Pythia spans the gap between intellect and body, fusing them into a whole integer. In like manner, a new unity in Ion is formed: "There is a third Ion to be born from the struggle of these two . . . a spirit yet a man. . . . From Ion the spirit and Ion the mortal, is born a third, compound of man and god, Ion, the Ionian." Ion has attained identity; out of the two has come one—another meaning of "Ion." As with Hippolytus, this new self is realized only through *agon*, by means of division and conflict: "this birth, like all birth, is physically painful, and spiritually heart-breaking." As consciousness dawns, Ion reacts to the words of the Pythia ("mother of my spirit") with a shying away from the light: "O, day, O, too luminous." Ion is prevented from knowingly accepting "second-best": he is forced into self-realization. "At the exact second, as his hand reached out, and his material body was to be sworn-in as it were, to a brotherhood of mastery and battle, the hand drops. There is a greater brotherhood. He does not yet know this." It is Kreousa who jolts him to awareness of the transcendent. The truth of Ion's paternity is the divine; an affliction which disrupts all security: "He too, in a moment, would be dragged back into this psychic hinterland of loss, doubt, loss of personal identity, loss of mundanity, loss of material position, that terrible groping depersonalization of all true sons of the sun-god, music, and inspiration." His inheritance is the over-conscious burden of art.

V

APOLLO, the father-god, eschews a direct epiphany; in his place, his "sister" Athene, *"deus ex machina* steps forth":

> . . . intellect, mind, silver but shining with so luminous a splendour that the boy starts back, confusing this emanation of pure-spirit with that other, his spirit-father . . . this most beautiful abstraction of antiquity and of all time, pleas for the great force of the under-mind or the unconscious that so often, on the point of blazing upward into the glory of inspirational creative thought, flares, by a sudden law of compensation, down, making for tragedy, disharmony, disruption, disintegration, but in the end, O, in the end, if we have patience to wait . . . if we have penetration and faith and the desire actually to follow all those hidden subterranean forces, how great is our reward.

So reassures "the shining intellect, standing fully armed." Entelechy brings all things to culmination. In the setting sun, silver is transformed to gold. The human and divine interpenetrate, conjoin, separate; "these warm people who yet remain abstraction."

Mother unites with son—"the woman who is queen and almost goddess, who now in her joy wishes to be nothing but the mother of Ion." The gulf between the abstract and the human has been bridged. Kreousa is mother not only of the boy Ion, but of a new culture as well, the product of conjoined opposites (symbolized by Ion's newly born wholeness), "the welding of strength and delicacy":

> The mother, if she but knew it, of a new culture, of an aesthetic drive and concentrated spiritual force, not to be reckoned with, in terms of any then known values. . . . For this new culture was content, as no culture had been before, or has since been, frankly with one and but one supreme quality, perfection. Beyond that, below it and before it, there was nothing. The human mind dehumanized itself, in much the same way (if we may imagine group-consciousness so at work) in which shell-fish may work outward to patterns of exquisite vari-

ety and unity. The conscious mind of man had achieved kinship with unconscious forces of most subtle definition . . . had yet one fundamental inner force that framed them, projected them. . . .

Even though fully armed, the tender olive-shoot of this new culture needs to be nurtured: "incredibly frial, incredibly silver, it reached toward the light." The outward embodiment of its strength is the projected symbol of the column: "Now sharp Ionic columns start up, shafts of unblemished marble point the way to a return; worship the eternal. Indestructible beauty lives."

With the setting of the sun, events have come full cycle; the crumbled stones of Delphi—"the façade to lie among thistles, the gold to be fouled and tarnished by lizard, snail and the serpent"—yet emanate light. The spirit survives: "While one Ionic column stands, stark white and pure on the earth, that name shall live, the power of the goddess shall not have passed. . . ."

VI

For H. D., *Ion* formed part of a trilogy of oracle plays ("a defamed or 'lost' oracle") by Euripides—along with *Helen in Egypt* and *Iphigenia*—which together composed an Eleusinian cycle. Stages of initiation; levels of mental strata: sub-conscious, conscious, super-conscious; gradations of psychic progression: physical, intellectual, visionary; the ripening of wholeness—these are some of the connotations that the Eleusinian mysteries held for H. D. (*cf.* "Notes on Thought and Vision"). Eleusis revealed the mystery of the spontaneous growth of the spirit as the nurturing of a plant:

> Because the spirit, we realise, is a seed. No man by thought can add an inch to his stature, no initiate by the strength and power of his intellect can force his spirit to grow.
>
> He cannot force his spirit to grow, but he can retard its growth. At least so it seems to me.
>
> He can retard its growth by neglect of his body because the body of man as the body of nature is the ground into which the seed of spirit is cast.
>
> This is the mystery of Demeter, the Earth Mother. The body of the

Eleusinian initiate had become one with the earth, as his soul had become one with the seeds enclosed in the earth.

In the rites of Eleusis, mother and daughter are reunited, after separation, loss and sorrow, now forming a complementary harmony. In the ritual, the buried seed sprouts; a golden shaft of wheat emerges from the dead earth. In H. D.'s versions (i.e., *Hippolytus Temporizes* and *Ion*), it is the son who is reunited with the mother: "Christ and his father, or as the Eleusinian mystic would have said, his mother, were one."

In *Ion* familiar preoccupations of H. D. appear: the unknown father—transcendent god or human surrogate; a young man's search for identity, linked with the quest for knowledge of his paternity; the young man's dedication to his vocation as priest-artist; the rival claims of matriarchy and patriarchy; the growth toward wholeness, reconciling the contrasts between spirit and body; the awareness of a psychic pattern in events. *Ion* had a deeply personal significance for H. D., as is witnessed by her excited, enthusiastic entry in "Compassionate Friendship": "This little room that Bryher had the last time she was here [Villa Verena], will always be vibrating with the *Ion* broadcast that we heard there, in the dark the Tuesday of Xmas week." This B.B.C. radio transmission of the play from London—arranged by Norman Holmes Pearson—possessed importance enough for H. D. to inscribe in a copy of *Ion* the following:

	Broadcast	— London
	Dec. 19	— 3 p.m.
	Dec. 21	— 9 p.m.
heard	— Küsnacht	— 1954 —
		4 p.m.
		10 p.m.

The precise notation of dates and times are characteristic of H. D.'s recording of events of import, turning-points of significance. Elsewhere in "Compassionate Friendship" H. D. again refers "to the *Ion* that I worked on so many years and finally heard Christmas week, a broadcast from London." For exactly how long

H. D. had worked on *Ion* is somewhat unclear; on a page-proof of the first printing there is noted: "*Ion:* 1935—Assembled Vaud, Switzerland from rough notes begun in England 1915–1917 and Greece 1920 & 1932," while "Autobiographical Notes" reads: "1917: Started work on *ION* in Devon." Regardless of the exact starting point, *Ion* was a long period in gestation before attaining final form (as was the case with several other works).

The full significance which the broadcast held for H. D. remains, of necessity, deeply complex. The completing of *Ion* (1935) came at a time in H. D.'s life during which she experienced the sense of release from a stifling psychological blockage. Having ended a set of psychoanalytic sessions with Freud, H. D. perhaps considered the completion of her work on *Ion* as a weaving together of lost threads of her poetic identity, as a symbol of restored wholeness and balance? H. D. believed that the bringing of the play into final form would "break the backbone of my H. D. repression." In finalizing it, H. D. was asserting the validity of her identity as a poet: "I am, I am, I AM a Poet," while at the same time affirming her priestess dedication to the Delphic oracle (*cf.* Barbara Guest, *Herself Defined*). The broadcast, coming as it did at a later period of crisis, served to again confirm her identity as true artist; a fact publicly verified though the objective, external rendering of her personal visionary voice via the mechanism of radio transmission.

The *Ion* also linked H. D. back to her trip with Bryher to Delphi and Corfu in 1932. The original dedication to the play reads: "To Bryher Macpherson and Perdita Macpherson, Athens 1920–Delphi 1932." It was during that 1932 trip that H. D. came into contact again with the ever-living, tangible Hellenic symbol: "we touched the stem of a frail sapling, an olive-tree, growing against the egg-shell marble walls of the Erechtheum." It was also during this trip that she recorded the following disjointed observations: "Artemis too, rites of human sacrifice—a mother—versus—anti and un Dorian . . . —single white—rock—rose and iron-red rock—rose Artemis! human sacrifice—tall white, heath-cold rain—then sleet, steel-cold-grey-rock—Artemis! Bracken in cactus hedge!" ("Autobiographical Notes"). If H. D. had once projected her identity into the persona of Artemis (a prominent figure in *Hippolytus Temporizes*), she registers here the stark awareness of the goddess' inhumanity. (It is to be remembered that it is to Artemis that Iphigenia is to be sacrificed.) Remarks by both Freud (that H. D. was "not really interested . . . in humanity") and Harriet Monroe ("she is quite unconsciously, a lithe, hard, bright-winged spirit of nature to whom humanity is but an incident") served to point up in H. D.'s mind the resemblance between herself and the virgin goddess. Might not Kreousa, "the woman . . . who now in her joy wishes to be nothing but the mother of Ion," and Athene, "the smiling, ironical, thin and fragile goddess" of intellect—uniting the human and the transcendent—now be indicative of a newly formed balance between duality, replacing a one-sided absoluteness? In completing *Ion*, might the ice not have thawed: "that your heart may be free"?

—*John Walsh*

NOTE ON THE TEXT

In 1954 H. D. reread her *Ion* translation, and the present text incorporates the emendations H. D. then made in her copy of the 1937 printing (published by Chatto & Windus), subsequently given to Norman Holmes Pearson and presently in the Collection of American Literature, Beinecke Rare Book and Manuscript Library, Yale University—whose courteous help is thankfully noted.

NOTES ON EURIPIDES (excerpts)

. . . some of Euripides' most exquisite love-lyrics perished with his great Love drama. . . . Those lyrics were stained with ineffable purity we do know and we may be sure with underlying psycho-physical intensity.

Such a play might even have risen to the spiritual-emotional heights of the Ionians. . . .

Is it not possible that the later censure that precluded so many of the most exquisite stanzas of Sappho, in like manner forbade these [love lyrics]? . . . Many of Euripides' surviving plays hold outright anti-war and anti-social protest. But erotic-emotional innovation is comparatively rare. An interesting point rises, is his real personal philosophy lost, what did these plays contain, how did they approach life? Surely, in some ultra-modern spirit if the surviving plays are any clue to the lost ones. Euripides was unpopular during his life as a free-thinker, and an iconoclast. It is save to assume that the lost plays held pertinent modern matter.

. . . Euripides lived through almost a modern great-war period. . . . How would 1917 London have acclaimed such anti-war propaganda? Work that out and you will have some idea of the power and detachment of the Attic dramatist. For we are too apt to pigeon-hole the Attic poets and dramatists, put them B.C. this or that, forget them in our survey of modern life and literature, not realizing that the whole spring of all literature (even of all life) is that one small plane-leaf of an almost-island, that tiny rock among the countries of a world, Hellas.

Look at the map of Greece. Then go away and come back and look and look and look at it. The jagged contours stir and inflame the imagination, time-riddled banner of freedom and fiery independence, a rag of a country, all irregular, with little torn-off bits, petals drifting, those islands, "lily on lily that o'er lace the sea." Look at the map of Greece. It is a hieroglyph. You will be unable to read it and go away and come back after years and just begin to spell out the meaning of its outline. Then you will realize that you know nothing at all about it and begin all over, learning a cryptic language. I am never tired of speculating on the power of that outline, just the mysterious line of it, apart from the thing it stands for. That leaf hanging a pendant to the whole of Europe seems to indicate the living strength and sap of the thing it derives from. Greece is indeed the tree-of-life, the ever-present stream, the spring of living water. . . .

. . . the lines of this Greek poet (and all Greek poets if we have but the clue) are today as vivid and as fresh as they ever were, but vivid and fresh not as literature (though they are that too) but as portals, as windows, as portholes I am tempted to say that look out from our ship our world, our restricted lives, on to a sea that moves and changes and bears us up, and is friendly and vicious in turn. These words are to me portals, gates.

I know that we need scholars to decipher and interpret the Greek, but we also need: poets and mystics and children to re-discover this Hellenic world, to see *through* the words; the word being but the outline, the architectural structure of that door or window, through which we are all free, scholar and unlettered alike, to pass. We emerge from our restricted minds (with all due reverence to them, of course) into a free, large, clear, vibrant, limitless realm, sky and sea and distant islands, and a shore-line such as this in Egypt and another along the coast of Asia Minor or further toward the Bosphorus, and again Greece, Hellas, the thousand intimate bays, the foaming straits.

The Opening Scenes of Ion

I

THIS PLAY of Euripides opens as is customary, with a long prologue. The prologue (apart from the beauty of the language) is in itself a rather tedious affair. As most people who read Greek a little, start, as is natural, at the beginning of a play, they are as naturally bored, and usually do not finish the prologue and conclude forever after if they are honest, that a Greek play is a bore. Or if they continue and finish, they are depressed throughout the drama, by the memory of the struggle and the weight of that ponderous beginning. The beginning is meant to be ponderous, it is more or less purposely boring.

The chief characters are named; the plot as in a grand-opera programme, briefly outlined.

The Athenian playgoer knew then from the start who would enter, what was about to take place. He came from his house, his regiment, from civic, social or political duties. "Of nothing, too much." The Athenian citizen was not to be jerked suddenly from one world to another. Life was to merge with art. But it was to merge, to be bridged gradually.

The long prologue was this bridge.

Though Attic tragedy was above all religious in purport, then (as in our own picture-theaters or grand-opera auditoriums) there must have been whisperings and shufflings and a general atmosphere of unrest at the beginning of a play.

Although we may visualize the actor, the speaker of the prologue, as having already entered, introducing himself as Hermes, the messenger, son of Maia and of the "greatest daemon, Zeus," the young aristocrat, Caierophon is in no way showing disrespect to the father of gods and men and to Hermes his offspring, in turning to salute his friend, the soldier Paralus three tiers above him, or in leaning to whisper informally to the companion at his side. "We are at Delphi, I presume."

Unquestionably the row of Doric pillars, set on a raised dais approached by four or five steps, before which the speaker of the prologue is standing, represents the famous temple of Phoebos. Caierophon scarcely listens to the words. His mind still concerned with the same problem of city-revenue, catches a phrase, a name here and there, as one of us, tired and a little bored, might still untangle an already familiar *motif* or *leit-motif* from an obscure Tristram or Siegfried overture, and at the same time, recall matters of the day, a gown tried on or a tea-party or its masculine equivalent, so-and-so at the club or I must find a new tailor. We, as Caierophon, must bridge life, art gradually.

Then as Caierophon's ears become accustomed to this melodious rhythm, he bends once more to a whisper, "our Euripides has condescended to the rabble, this fairy-tale is hardly suitable to so great an audience; it veils no doubt, some jibe at our distinguished contemporaries."

So far we may enter into the sophisticated mind of this most sophisticated and polished gathering the world has ever known. Then like children, we must follow simply the simple story outlined by the god Hermes, lord of the caduceus and of the sandals, "gold, rare, imperishable."

For the god is telling us that Helios, his brother, loved, as was customary among the Olympians, a maiden. This girl was Kreousa, descendant of Erechtheus, the mythical founder of Athens. She bore a child and in fear of her father, exposed it on the rocks. The god Helios, not quite ignoble, sends his brother Hermes to bring the baby, the basket he lies in, his clothes and little wrappings to the temple at Delphi. There the child lives as a young priest, with certain duties. Kreousa, his mother, marries Xouthos, a neighboring prince. They have no child. The queen and her husband make a pilgrimage to Delphi (a customary pilgrim-journey not unlike that undertaken in later times on various pretexts to Rome) to enquire of the God of prophecy as to their fortune. Kreousa is desperate, the old god-like race of Erechthonius ends with her death.

The voice of the actor rings clear now, whisperings have died away. The God, he explains, will give this very child to Xouthos, persuade him that it is his own; the boy shall enter his mother's palace, obtain his inheritance, yet keep secret the mystery of his birth.

We know in brief the story of the play, its beginning and its end.

Toward the back of the stage, half-hidden by the pillars, the young actor appears.

The speaker of the prologue turns: "but I see Helios' son approaches to sweep the porch with his laurel-branch." He steps toward the right. "I—and I first—call him by his own name—Ion."

II

THE BOY comes slowly down the steps. He wears a tunic, simply folded, embroidered with heavy work of gold thread. Perhaps as a young priest, he wore the tall boots, attribute of Helios, slayer of death and gloom in the Monster Python. From the words of the prologue just spoken we know that he carries a branch or small bundle of laurel-twigs.

At this moment if the Greek drama were grand-opera, the heavy, more or less ponderous and complex overture, the blending of many instruments, would evolve itself into one theme. If we were trained musicians we would have been aware of the alteration of mood about two-thirds through the speech of Hermes. But as god disappears, the notes become light, easy to follow. The main instruments are strings, notably the harp or *phorminx*, adopted by the God, accompaniment to inspired speech and prophetic utterance.

The boy comes slowly forward and pauses. The two lines of young priests who have entered from opposite sides, join in a single half-circle at the back of the stage below the temple pillars.

Ion lifts his laurel branch.

Armata men tade lampra tethrippon.

Hail chariot and chariot-driver, God about to step toward us over the untrodden peaks, to step down the mountain-passes toward us, your lovers, your children.

His words, the sound, the subtly accented rhythm, above all the swift bright flow, the movement of the whole, acts upon us, bears the same relation to our nerves, our nervous organism, as music, but is as far above ordinary music, we might be tempted to say, as music is above common speech.

There is no adequate translation for the Greek words and there never will be.

The mere skeleton runs something like this:

Helios' chariot
four-abreast,
fagot-torch,
sets fire to earth;
out of the ether,
stars flee from this star
into the holy night;
Parnassus'
unconquered heights
catch light while the sun-disc
swims into mortal sight
with myrrh
above the roof,
smoke
from dried incense-branch,
while on the Delphic seat
the high priestess waits
to chart the God's will
unto the Greeks.

We see with the eyes of the young actor, not the row of priests and officials, not the circle above them; writer, statesman, sculptor, Caierophon and Apollodorus, the whole body of aristocratic Athens, the well-born, the spiritually well-endowed, nor yet the mass of bourgeois, the Gastrons and Drekons, crowding tier on tier above them. But with the eyes of a young priest and with the eyes of a poet we see Parnassus, the mountain that has stood for just a second before actual dawn, black against the silver-grey of the false-dawn, in just that second become two peaks, jagged, in exquisite outline, until every detail becomes suddenly visible, and through the twin-peaks there pours a fire, pours and swirls upward, and the whole sky above is mad with the riot, and the runnels and channels and dried ditches of the rocky mountain are filled with gold.

The music of the lines, as an accompaniment of strings following a song may continue with light variation after the actual song
is finished, lingers, for a few beats, after the boy has finished
speaking.

Ion turns. Almost with a sharp voice, almost with the tones of a
chausseur urging forward the hounds, or that of the goal-keeper at
the moment when the charioteers drop their tense posture of
expectancy and the taut reins fall loose on the flanks of great
steeds, almost his voice takes such a clear deep resonance as he
turns to the row of youthful priests attending him.

> *Go,*
> *go Delphic priests,*
> *cleanse and purify your spirits*
> *in Kastalia's silver pool-depth;*
> *wholly purified, come back,*
> *speak as he would have you speak,*
> *word for word the mystic writ,*
> *soothsayers and holy prophets,*
> *unto those who seek*
> *his help.*

The boy pauses again, the priests have gone, the pattern, the
frieze one might almost say against which he has been standing,
is changed to another. The precise posture of the row of attending
youths (even although we have been but half-conscious of their
presence) has had the same effect upon our nerves, as a plaque in
low-relief against which some fine statue of the *duodemonos* or
young athlete might stand. But we become conscious of the fine
vigour of this *basso-relievo* only when the boy turns, only when he
himself notices it, leaving the single figure slight, intense and frail
against the great, ribbed pillar of the temple-portico.

He continues in a lower voice, as if explaining half to himself,
his position, his relative worth and his insignificance in face of the
emblems of worship surrounding him.

> *This is my work:*
> *even as a mere youth,*
> *with chaplet of flowers*
> *and laurel in the new leaf,*

I made fragrant the steps
and the threshold of Helios:
I sprinkled the pavement,
showering water-drops:
and with my swift darts
frightened the bird-flocks,
that would perch on the temple-gifts.
I put them to sudden flight:
fatherless, motherless,
alone in the temple-gates,
I praise Helios,
my source of life.

Then as if the god himself had touched him, as he rings from his own *phorminx* his own most lovely music, the boy is caught, torn from his quiet worship. He has become enraptured, one with the God, merged into him, fire of song, spark of a greater fire. He is Hyacinth whom the god loved. We close our eyes to shut out sound and the vision of our fellow-beings dark beside us, inert and stagnant, in their circle of stone-benches. But most of all to escape this vision, the boy caught, struggling, a white bird in a great wind, a flower, exposed to the sun.

Come, laurel,
beloved, most sweet,
(O shoot, leaf and new-leaf
 and flower, beautiful to sweep
 beneath altar, across pavement)
from flower-slopes
where gods walk:
where crystal streams,
swift water-paths
feed the roots
of holy myrtle-plants,
with whose branch too I sweep
precinct
pavement;
all day,
day-long I work
from the first dawn-hint
of the fire-wings,
I greet

Paion,
O Paion,
king,
priest;
may you be for ever blest,
Latona's child,
loveliest.

Ah, but the task is sweet,
cleaning your threshold, Phoebos,
worshipping the mysteries:
ah, but his task is slight
who serves a god,
a deathless spirit,
never weariness can touch
a servant of such rapture servant,
Helios is father-spirit:
hail, Helios, my pledge of life,
father, father, through the house
I speak your name
intent to worship

Paion,
O Paion,
king,
priest;
may you be for ever blest,
Latona's child,
loveliest.

He pauses. The boy reaches toward the flask or jar of beaten gold, which stands on one of the upper steps, its shape, half-lost in the shadow beneath the pillar.

Ion lifts the jar, holds it in the curve of one arm. With stiff, precise movements (perfect in rhythm with the turn of the head) he scatters spray on spray of water into the open porch of the temple and across the steps below him.

Now I must finish this,
drop my laurel-branch,
take the pitcher,
this golden flask of water,

fresh as when the earth
sprayed it from Kastalia's rocks;
I, a spirit, unharassed,
scattering the sacred drops,
pray: Helios, may I never cease
this service but for gracious death.

What is this note of death? It seems from the bright exultation of the boy's voice to refer to some knowledge, to hint of some joy, guessed at or actually experienced in the mysteries of the inner worship to which he has perhaps gained admittance, sanctioned as foster-child and favourite of the priests and of the god.

But we have not time to speculate on this for the boy starts from his reverie, places his jar once more upon the step and with a sudden movement reaches for a tall bow standing against the pillar.

With a shout he bounds down the steps. Is some Python about to rear a black head from among the bays where Hermes has lately hid himself, or some barbarian, enemy to beauty, rush out from the bushes? But no, we gather from the movement of the head and the bending of the slender throat that it is something in the air above that has startled Ion.

Birds,
you dart from Parnassus,
then back to Parnassus;
you rest on the roof,
the roof-peak, the gold cornice;
ah legate of Zeus,
tyrant of small flocks:
this match for claw and beak
my arrow threatens—
swift, be off.

O swan,
O slow-drifting next,
O bird of the scarlet feet,
is no other place fair enough,
but this, but his holiest,
no marsh-land
no field of Delos?

Ah swift,
for the song-note,
tuned to the god's bright phorminx,
cannot heal, O bird,
a blood-stained throat.

What fluttering—
a new bird this,
and she, actually she rests,
with wisps of straw
beneath the cornice;
my bow repeats the threat,
be off, lest grass and twigs
should litter up
the offerings set about the porch;
my arrow warns you;
rather hatch your brood
along the river Alpheus,
or further yet,
in Isthmian thickets.
Be off—I must do my work,
my duty to the gods and priests.

but birds, birds,
how can I hurt
you, messengers,
God's voice on earth.

We seem to hear through the movement and power of the Greek words, the whirr of swift arrows, the fluttering of many wings. And we wonder what birds these are that the boy sees in his imagination; this "new bird" that he speaks of, was it some rare crane or ibis flying from Egypt across the desert and the Corinthian-gulf, that had once startled the poet with blue-black gleam of its velvet throat and its spotted wings, as he visited Delphi, and as a child perhaps, escaped from the temple to follow the flare of colour against the mountain, to watch the flight of some flamingo-like bird, fire against the pinnacle of fire?

III

THE BOY rests on an upper step beneath one of the great side-pillars and we lose sight of him momentarily, as a group of women enter from the opposite side.

These ladies are not inmates of the temple. We judge from the elaborate blending of gold and silver ornaments, the fine braiding of hair, the well-chosen and costly garments, that they are women of some worldly standing. From the first words of the speaker we learn that they are Athenians.

> *Not in Athens where the gods walk,*
> *are the porches set about,*
> *pillar by pillar*
> *with more beautiful work,*
> *nor shrines before the highways*
> *for their worship:*
> *but here, too at the seat*
> *of the God-prophet, Latona begot,*
> *light strikes beauty*
> *from twin-wrought temple-fronts.*

They are astonished at the beauty of the temple. They separate, two by two, or one wanders alone to examine closely the paintings beyond the pillars, set, we are led to believe, in the inner-porch. We cannot see these pictures but from the informal conversation of these women, we can almost reconstruct line from line the paintings, perhaps imagined of the poet (himself a painter in youth) or else graphically described from sketches seen in the atelier of some friend or from the finished work intended to stand on the Acropolis (as yet unrecovered from the attack of the Persians) still in the hands of architect and sculptor.

> *Here, see the son of Zeus,*
> *look—my friend—bend close—*
> *threatens with a golden knife*
> *the snake of the Lernian marsh.*

These stately women become eager, excited—"see—see," drawing attention to this, to that detail as they recall early friezes perhaps remembered as children in some small rustic temple in the environs of Athens, or some detail of a god's life they stitched as young girls in Athens' temple-porches.

> *Yes, yes, and near it,*
> *another lifts a bright torch,*
> *who is it—I have wrought*
> *his deeds across my distaff—*
> *ah, he who took the god's hurt*
> *sharing his dire grief,*
> *the spearsman, Iolaus.*

> *Ah this—but see this,*
> *a youth on a winged horse,*
> *is slaying a monstrous beast*
> *three-bodied with fiery breath.*

> *We gaze about—see—*
> *across the walls of rock,*
> *the rout of the earth-born giants.*

So they pass from picture to picture. And I should be inclined to believe that the poet had in mind some series, highly decorative, in low relief—rather than paintings—for we notice he has not once employed that so marvellous word *kuaneas*, the Greek blue, nor any hint of saffron nor purple-black shadows such as Pindar, for example, uses in his famous passage, descriptive of the birth of this very Ion. But there is everywhere gold. We follow the gesture of the Athenian woman, surprising in each inset, some glitter of gold-leaf or ornament of dark gold. From the metallic gleam of Heracles' scimitar, our eyes trace the intricate, decorative twisting of the dragon and with the slash of its tail are led upward to gold again, the torch held aloft by the young hero, Iolaus. Perhaps dripping of gold sparks leads our eyes down again to wonder at the head of the next beast, "fire-breathing": once more the fire is gold.

> *We note this—*

> *She shakes an aegis,*
> *dragon-wrought,*
> *threatening Enkeladous.*

> *Ah, Pallas, my goddess!*

Fire this and fire-bolt,
in the far-reaching hands of Zeus.

So from the gold or brass, gleaming, we may imagine, from the barbaric bracelets on the fore-arms of the giants, we are drawn from a raised fore-arm to the circle of the great shield which the mighty Titaness brandishes, Athené, the goddess.

The shield-rim is set in gold and there is gold again in the lightning-spears of Zeus and a gold head-band, we might imagine, about the head of the peaceful Dionysus. They pause together before the last picture.

With his fire-shaft he strikes,
shattering the giant, Mimos,
and Bromios, the glad heart,
with ivy-staff (not meant for this)
slays another child of earth.

They turning, they find the boy Ion seated on the steps.

IV

HE HAS RISEN now and stands.

He, as servant of the temple is accustomed to the sight of strangers, the drift of pilgrims of all classes and all countries. And he regards the leader of the band as she steps forward, calmly without special interest.

She asks him if they may enter the temple.

"No," he says and adds, "it is not customary."

"May we converse then, with you, one of the temple servants?"

"That, yes—what is it?"

"Is it true that Helios' temple really does rest on the very heart of the earth?"

He answers "indeed yes"—fragrant with garlands—offerings of scented flowers, laurels and azaleas and great mass and spike of flowers from mountain-bush and tree—and he adds "dragons watch it."

"Such was the common tale," the Athenian lady answers, anxious now that the boy should realise them as not quite ignorant of the temple and temple-myth.

He sees now that these are no ordinary sight-seers and he unbends a little, telling them of the custom of sacrificing before entering the temple, bloodless sacrifice, the archaic wheat, honey and oil-cake, but after, real blood-sacrifice is required if they intend to visit the inner-shrine.

The woman thanks him, saying they will transgress no sacred custom, but wait outside and examine further the beautiful detail of the porches.

"Do so, by all means," and the woman answers that their mistress has always wanted them to see this.

"Of what house are you called servants?"

> *Our mistress is of Athens;*
> *the porches of Pallas are her court—*
> *you ask of her—she is present.*

V

SHE HAS ENTERED unnoticed this tall woman, Kreousa, child of Erechtheus, queen of Athens. And she stands, motionless, a statue almost wrought of lapis, we might think, so intense a blue is her robe, falling in straight folds to her feet.

The boy moves toward her, but she does not speak.

The attendant-women scatter silently through the porches and disappear.

Again the boy moves, wondering at the strange, intense beauty of this face. And still she does not speak or turn, her eyes on the temple-porch.

"O noble, of most noble birth" the boy begins, he, the child and fosterling of the temple, nameless, humble before this presence, falters, waits and then:

> *O noble of birth,*
> *beautiful in appearance,*
> *you have that look,*
> *whoever you are, O woman,*
> *that most men, seeing your face*
> *would know*
> *you were sprung of a great people;*
> *but what is this—*
> *it comes as a shock to me,*

those half-shut eyes, staining with tears
that proud face,
even after you have looked
at the altar of Helios.

Oh lady,
with what thought do you approach,
for most, seeing the god's house,
laugh out—only you
weep at the sight.

She turns, the rapt face softens, the statue's face changed into a woman's as she becomes conscious of this other, its youth and austere charm. As if speaking aloud her thoughts, she answers, impelled by some unquestionable power, some strange rapport between them.

Fair lad,
it is not unplaced
that you wonder seeing me weep,
but as I look upon this, Helios' house,
old memory stabs afresh,
and though standing here,
I am, as it were, alone
in my own place,
and I think:
how wretched, how miserable we women are,
what sport for fate—yet what of this?
how can we expect man's justice,
we who perish by gods' injustice
and their hate.

He, accustomed to tales of sorrow, confidence of pilgrim and invalid seeking consolation in the famous shrine of healing, easily enters into her mood and would soften her bitterness.

He draws near and inquires simply: "why are you hurt, tortured and sad?"

As I had intended to outline only the opening chorus of the *Ion*, I should have concluded with the last words of the waiting women before the entrance of the queen. For the whole character of the play alters after her coming. The boy's faith is shadowed. We are plunged into political discussions, religious doubts and curious rather crude plot and counter-plot.

But it was hard to turn away. The queen was standing there a moment ago, in her blue garments. All of his queens are beautiful and there are others of Euripides' women that are robed in blue. Thetis especially I see, as she appears in the last scene of the *Andromeda*. But her robe is another blue, a gentian or hyacinth-blue, an unworldly, unearthly colour. But Kreousa, queen of Athens, wears the blue of stones, lapis-blue, the blue of the fire in the earth, a blue that seems to symbolize not only her pride and her power but also her passion and her loss.

BLACK SWAN BOOKS
Literary Series

- ☐ H. D., *Bid Me to Live*
- ☐ H. D., *Hedylus*
- ☐ H. D., *Hippolytus Temporizes*
- ☐ H. D., *Ion*
- ☐ LAWRENCE DURRELL, *The Ikons*
- ☐ D. H. LAWRENCE, *Ten Paintings*
- ☐ ADRIAN STOKES, *With All the Views*
- ☐ VERNON WATKINS, *Unity of the Stream*
- ☐ W. B. YEATS, *Byzantium* (ill.)
- ☐ MICHAEL HAMBURGER, *Variations*
- ☐ PETER WHIGHAM, *Things Common, Properly*
- ☐ PETER RUSSELL, *All for the Wolves*
- ☐ PETER JONES, *The Garden End*
- ☐ RALPH GUSTAFSON, *At the Ocean's Verge*
- ☐ EZRA POUND / JOHN THEOBALD, *Letters*

Catalogue available